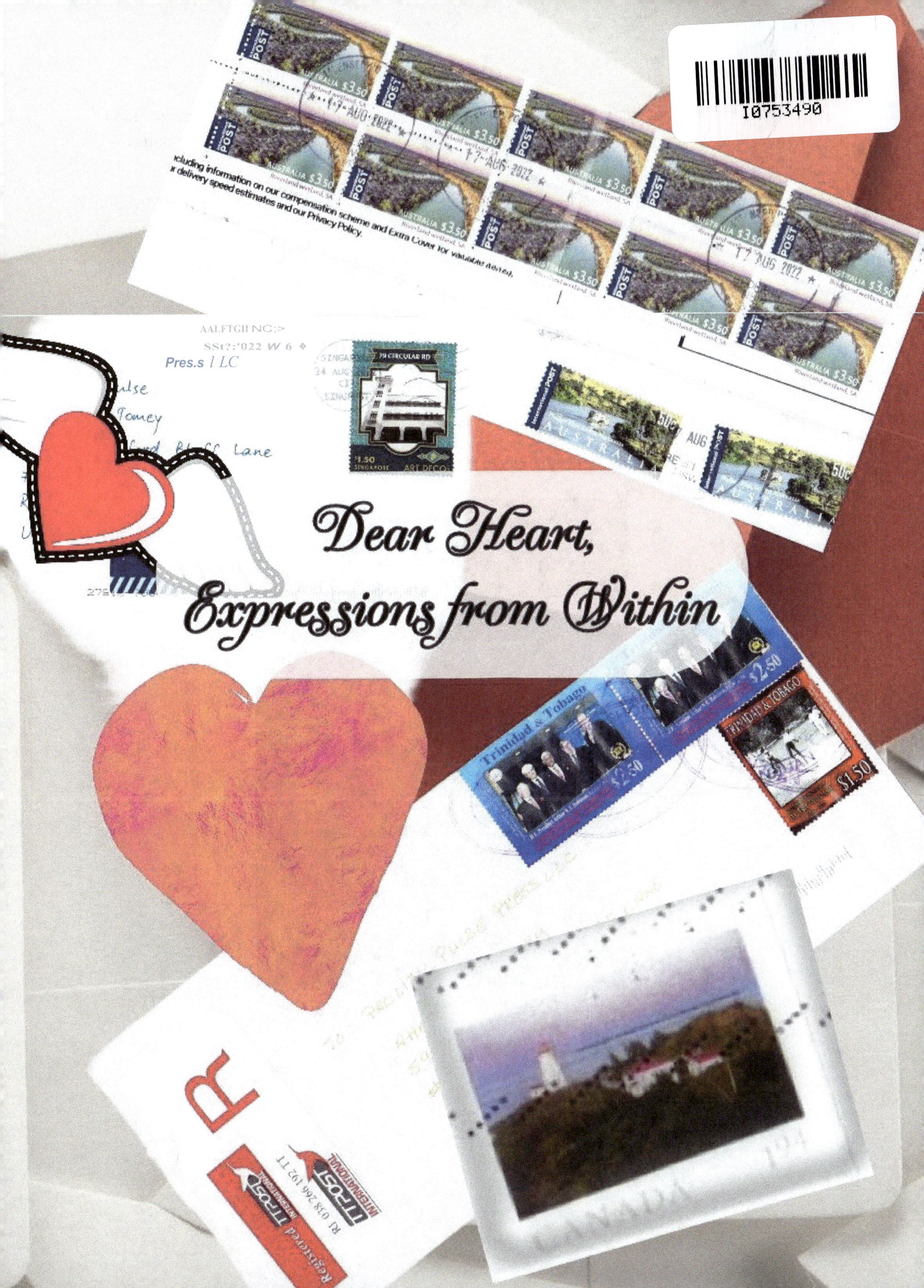
Dear Heart,
Expressions from Within

Published by Prolific Pulse Press LLC, Lisa Tomey-Zonneveld, Manager, Editor in Chief Co-

Co-Editor: Zaneta Varnado Johns

Cover Art: Kay Doiron

Other Compiler: Jodi Lynn Nehring ISBN:

978-1-962374-02-6

Published September 2023, Raleigh, North Carolina USA

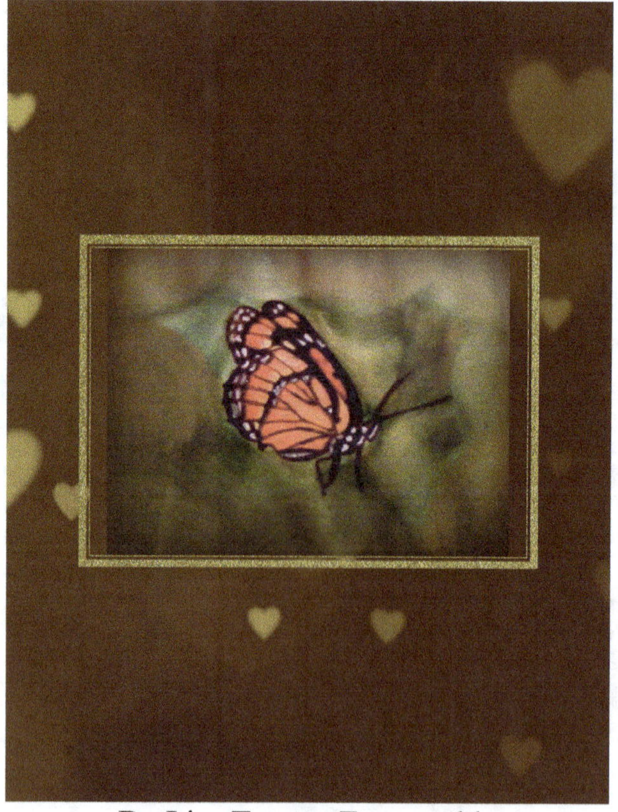

By Lisa Tomey-Zonneveld

Introduction

Before computers, we wrote letters. My mother's letters were like little novellas, several pages long. Her family members and friends loved to get her "books." Letters from mom were heartfelt and brought tears of love. As her pen moved passionately across the pages, sometimes her clear, blue eyes would well up.

Letters were her release. They were her way of expressing herself in ways she could not voice. Occasionally, she would write letters to people out of anger and then tear them up. These could have been to politicians, relatives, and those are the ones I knew about. She would express her heart's desire, open up her soul, and pour out her thoughts.

While I did not have the beautiful penmanship of my mother, I learned that the pen was my power. Some of my letters were releases which I destroyed. At age 15, I even wrote one about the need for a doctor in our little town. The letter and story was published in the newspaper.

As a writer and a poet, I write as if my words are letters to the world, perhaps to express the desires of my heart. Other times I write to simply write.

When we do express our desires within our heart, this has a way of stirring up thoughts and even action plans to make things happen. They could be acceptances of things that can't be changed, but often are steps toward courage to make something happen.

I posed this question and requested to others: *What is the desire in your heart? This is my challenge to you. I would like to read about the desires in your heart in the "Dear Heart" anthology of letters, poetry, art, photography, and whatever ways helps you express your passion.*

There was a caveat to this. In honor of my mother, the expressions were to be sent to me via good old fashioned snail mail.

Now, it is my pleasure to bring to you these beautiful heartfelt responses via *Dear Heart*.

Lisa Tomey-Zonneveld

Table of Contents

August 21, 2022

To my dearest sister, Janet,

Remember that feeling you get when you want something to eat, but you don't know what to eat? You look in the cupboards and refrigerator and nothing is appealing. You try eating this and that and your hunger isn't satisfied.

That's exactly how I feel at this moment. Except it's words I want to write. Stories I want to tell. There's an abundance to choose from. I just don't know which ones to put to paper.

To be completely honest, there's so many words and stories that

Alice Taylor

they're beyond any coherent thought. They're jumbled and bottle-necked in a pile just beyond my reach. It makes sense that this happened. After all, it's been almost fourteen years. Fourteen!

I shake my head as I think of this. We talked every day, sometimes for hours. Words were never a problem for us. There wasn't anything we couldn't talk about.

I still have the letter you gave to me. In a time of email and social media, you chose to write to me and deliver it by hand. You didn't like your handwriting. You typed in cursive font and then printed it.

I pulled the letter out of my wallet today to look at one more time. Something I haven't done for a very long time. You wrote it to me fifteen years ago for your fortieth birthday. In the letter you asked me not to cry. To this day I have shed tears every time I read it.

The letter is so tattered now that I'm afraid to open and read it again. The edges are frayed and the folds threaten to tear if I dare to open the letter one more time. I can't help but think that this single sheet of paper, meant to express your heart and soul, also reflects my heart and soul perfectly.

It still hurts immensely to even just think about you. About whom we were together. The words I could write to you today remain silent for me. Perhaps the pain would still be too much. Would the stories I could share bring me back into the incredibly deep sadness I experienced?

Sometime, what I imagine to be within days of your fatal car accident, I wrote the words...

My biggest fear is that I will feel this way for the rest of my life. My second biggest fear... is that I won't.

I don't remember writing those words. I didn't find them until a few years later. They were written on a pad of paper in my scrapbooking room. A room frozen in time. The photos from my fiftieth birthday still spread across my desk. It took about a decade for me to be able to even pick up my camera again. To this day it's still a rare occurrence.

The scrapbooking room is now my library.

Nothing is the same for me anymore. I'm still existing, not living, somewhere between my biggest and second biggest fears.

The words you wrote in your letter to me so many years ago are still true for me today. These words especially stood out for me... "I want you to know that you are always with me no matter where I am or what I'm doing." I had them inscribed on your headstone.

There are so many stories to share, so many words tumbling, desperately wanting to be included. It simply hurts too much to write them. Only because they're about experiences that should have been shared with you... when they were lived.

Love always,

Your loving sister, Alice

To My Dearest Sister Alice,

I know that you are not expecting this letter... so no crying after you read this because I'm there right now with you and I don't want to cry too!! I'm taking this opportunity of our day together (for my 40th birthday) to say some things that I can't always say (because I'll cry!)

Alice I miss you so much! And I really want to get together more often than we have. Remember I asked you not to cry!

We have been through so much together... good & bad times in the past 24 years or so, but we have never let go of each other as sisters, true friends and always have had at strong bond between us that no one can touch. I know we will always have this!

I want you to know that you are always with me no matter where I am or what I'm doing! When I'm going through those hard times I have in my life, I know your only a phone call away and I can always count on you for the morale support you have always given me. Your honesty, respect and caring way for me is more than I could ever ask for. Although I don't say this much but I know you already know this... I love you very much and nothing can change that. I hope that you will always know that I will always be there for you ; no matter what!

Alice , one last thing I have to say is... I am so proud to say that you are my closest friend & sister. In all my life I have never felt closer or let some one get this close to me, to know me as well as you do! Today is going to be a very special day for me , one that I will never forget... because I'm spending it with you!!

Love Always,

Your Loving Sister Janet

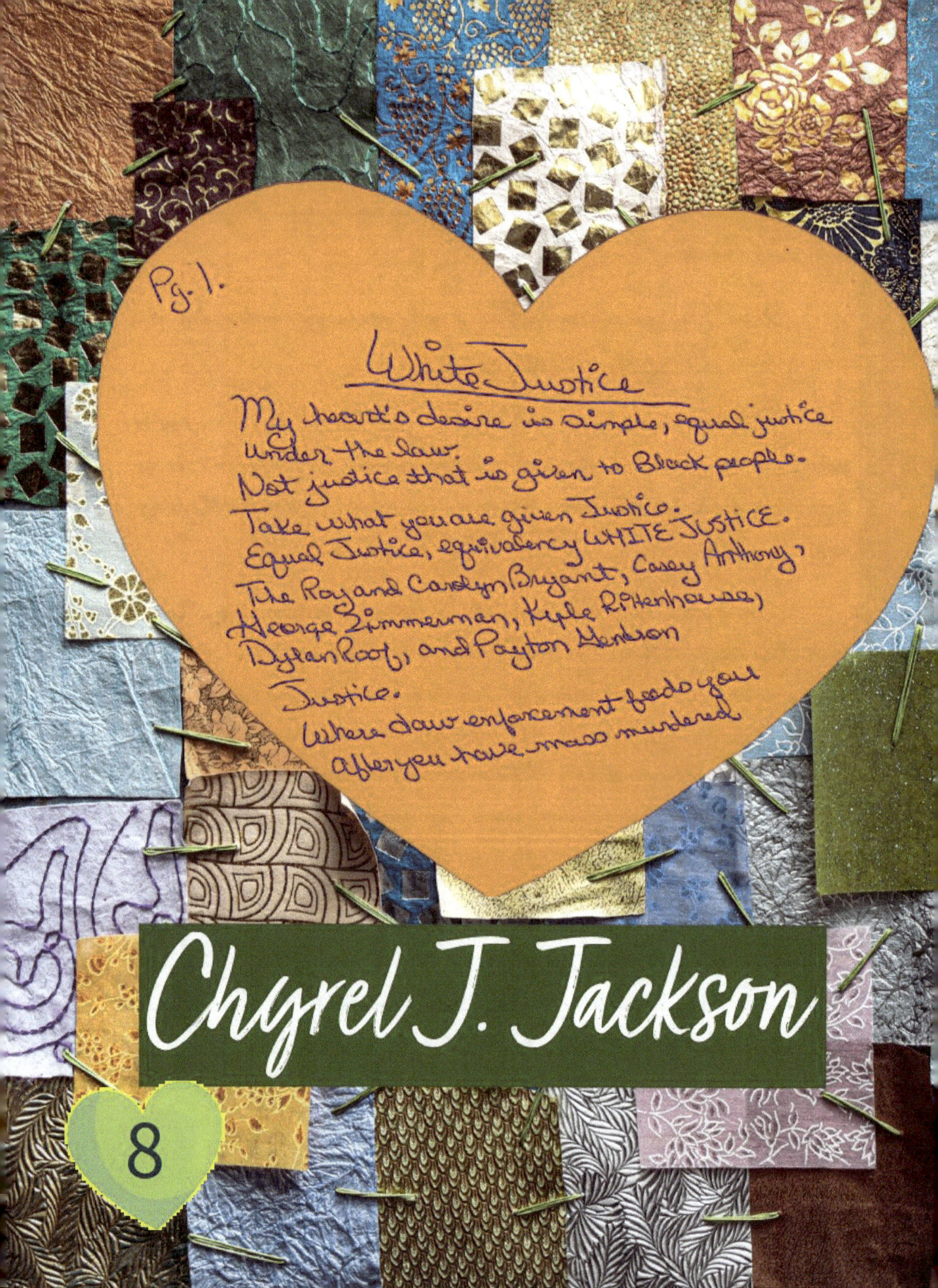
Pg. 1.
White Justice
My heart's desire is simple, equal justice
under the law.
Not justice that is given to Black people.
Take what you are given Justice.
Equal Justice, equivalency WHITE JUSTICE.
The Roy and Carolyn Bryant, Casey Anthony,
George Zimmerman, Kyle Rittenhouse,
Dylan Roof, and Payton Gendron
Justice.
Where law enforcement feeds you
After you have mass murdered
Chyrel J. Jackson
8

Pg. 2.

White Justice Continued...

multiple Black people.

The White Justice that gives you a hamburger the Way you want it, Burger No King, white Justice. My soul won't rest nor my heart's desire fulfilled until Black people like me, can experience complete exoneration of criminality equivalent to White Justice.

Until my 50+-year-old weary, bloodshot, eyes can witness Black people live White Justice.

There is no real Justice.

White people are not mowed down by police executi

Pg. 3.

White Justice Cont...

routine traffic Stops.

White people aren't executed in bed while sleeping.

Unless and until Black people can receive White Justice there can be no Equal JUSTICE.

My heart's desire, is to witness all Black lives receive White Justice.

Why can't Black people have the same consideration, assertion of presumed innocence, and sworn protection of police who serve and protect white lives?

No questions asked.

All lives do Not Matter.

Hence, the necessity of the Black Lives Matter mantra.

Pg. 4.

White Justice Cont...

All lives are not given equal value. Emmett Till and Breonna Taylor's life did not have the same value as the white murderers Roy/Carolyn Bryant, Kyle Rittenhouse, and Dylan Roof that walked away receiving WHITE JUSTICE.

That is simply a grotesque MISCARRIAGE OF JUSTICE.

I want White JUSTICE.

GJ

August 03, 2022

Dear Heart,

Over the years, my heart's desire has shifted like a rivers course, the one constant always being love.

A love that's pure, solid and yet malleable.

A love that grows not apart but seeks to nurture and be nurtured through the seasons.

A love that waits, that reciprocates, yielding and sparking with desire and laughter.

A love that persists in spite of egos, alas, a love that nestles nicely after storms.

I'm not asking for perfection, for I could never survive that infatuation but rather, something safe and honest, guiding one to the light when thoughts and moods draw dark.

I know I'm worth it, even if some days I don't believe it, for I am not always easy to hold, like a rose my thorns are real and I apologize profusely but I am worth it.

I have had to be strong for so long now, I want someone to hold in the silence of a love, extending like a pier beyond seeping fears.

Danielle Martin

I yearn to soften conversations with self, to cradle her and find some pieces that blew away on the journey leading to now.

I yearn to create a version of me that can give as well as receive this love my heart desires, transcending and radiating throughout and about today, tomorrow, and in the many moon cycles that my life may have yet to enjoy.

My heart's desire stretches to enfold the baby swaddled almost a score ago. May he find his own path bathed in wisdom and success. I know I won't always be here but I want him to know that I'll be there always, amongst the twinkling stars or in the warmth of a breeze when there is no wind.

Yes, my heart's desire is love, in this form and in the next, so just be aware for my love never ends, never abandons. It moves like Mother Nature, so also be aware there is no curtailing this heart's desire.

Love Always,
Danielle Martin.

15 Aug 2022

My Beloved Past,

How frightened were you when you witnessed your protectors' laying hands on each other? How helpless were you when you realised you couldn't defend grandma from grandpa's beating? How scared were you when your friends were punched and robbed right before your eyes? Violence made you timid and quiet, and your screams came out in all the wrong places. You walked with a hunched back as a teenager because of the weight of suffering in silence.

You loved strangers, they posed less threats than people who were close to you. You preferred distance than intimacy. You felt safe with your loved ones when there was a wall between you. You dared not to let them into your heart otherwise they would break into pieces as history had proven itself. You were filled with longing and yet so alone.

I know you danced alone, sang alone and cried alone. I know the trees knew your sorrow, the river knew your sadness, and the sky held your secrets. Before you met your Maker, you gained life from your Maker's creation. The wind raised

Jia-Li Yang

you to be strong as a tree; the rain nourished you to be healthy as a flower; the sun shined upon you to be blessed as the favourite one.

It was your Maker who loved you and granted you the ability to love. You were held by your Maker's hand and travelled back to those violent memories. You no longer faced them alone with weak knees. instead, you rose in your Maker's strength, with humility and compassion. You came to understand the violence was the outwork of human's corruption, and there was nothing you did to cause that. You were created in your Maker's image, pure and blameless.

There is so much I want to say to you. There is so much absence I want to make up for. There is so much love I want to express. And yet, without all these, you stand tall and beautiful. What's there left for me to say except 'I'm so proud of you!'?

Thank you for your existence. Thank you for reuniting with me. Thank you for making us whole again.

Love always,

Now

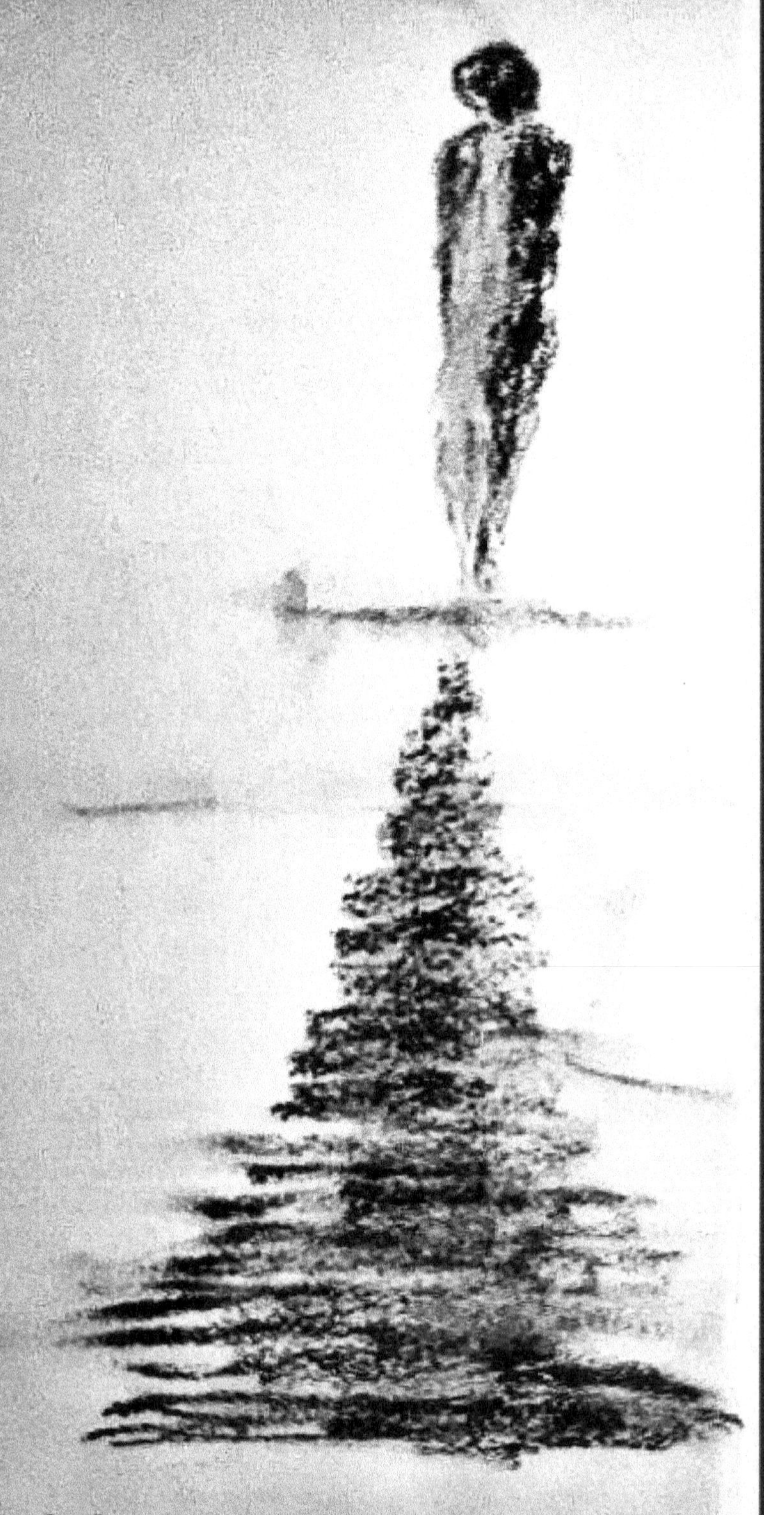
Lone shadow
Cassa Bassa Dec 2020

Dearest Cubby, 63rd birthday,

Sleep awhile more my love
your funny lopsided smile wrinkles
even as you rest

Those brown eyes register your dreams
as butterfly images dance with
enviable grace

I may never know of what you dream
shall always recall your peaceful gaze
soothing warmth where my lips
trailed kisses
upon the corners of your eyes
and soft berry lips

I am content to sit beside you
hands clasped, our breathing like a
metronome
a sweet synchronization

you call me, the one who awaits you return
home
"our enchanted cottage" ever more
beautiful
you have named our forever home

Jill Sharon Kimmelman

So many plans for shared adventures
what we ask each other to hold onto
what we ask ourselves to believe
and affirm

As I write upon these parchment pages
tears stain my cheeks
my palsied hands shake and quiver
I may have blotted a page or two
yet I take up my pen
determined to try again

Sleep awhile more my love
you remain my muse & my reason for
being
my forever love.

Love always,
Your Sugarbear

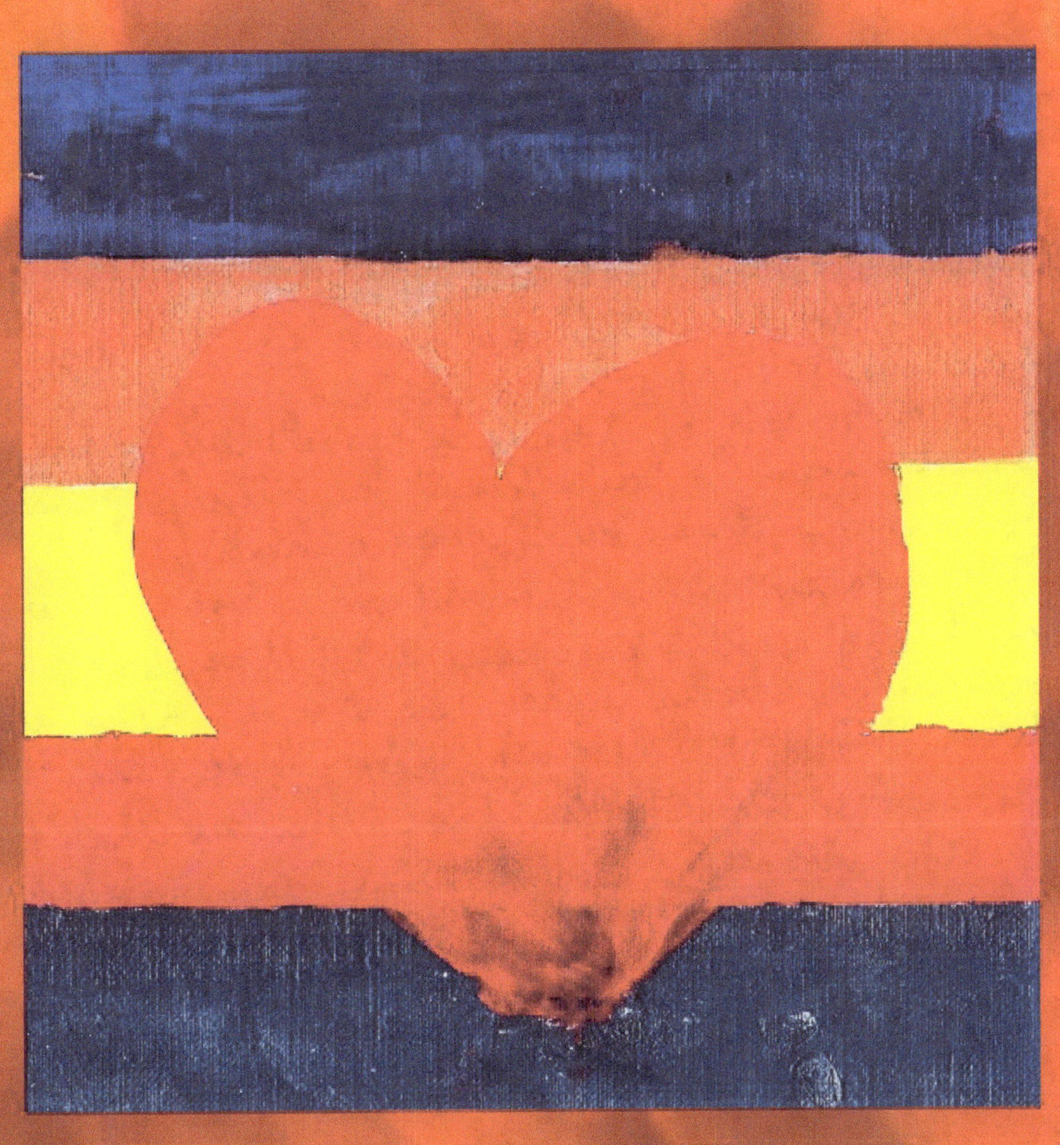

Jodi L. Nehring

Karen Monteith
Barrie, ON, Canada
August 28/2022

Annabella VanBerkel
Barrie ON, Canada

Dear Heart
From my heart to yours dear Annabella,

There are a few things I want to say that I would like you to remember as you go through your teen years and into adulthood.

I am so fortunate to have you as my granddaughter. You are a shining light in the family, a beacon of hope and possibility. You are not easily swayed and have a distinct mind of your own. These are good qualities!

I've watched you grow from a babe in arms to a lovely young woman who has so many opportunities being presented to you. You are athletic. You lead the way! Keep leading the way! Forge new ground! You have told us that hockey is a top priority. Follow your dream. I watch you... dedicated to your practice, lifestyle, nutrition and fitness. To perfect your shot, your skill and your game – you practice when there is not a formal session. You are always looking for ways to improve. I love that you are so focused.

You are brilliant and already know that you want to work in sport as a physio therapist or in another helping position.

Karen Monteith

Maintain your independence Bells by making your own choices and not following the crowd. Make decisions that are good for you and don't worry about what everyone else is doing.

I am so happy that you are nearby and that I feel close to you. I love when you send me text messages with little hearts. You make us matching bracelets. You painted an oilpainting for my birthday. I love it!

Your choices may change and that is perfectly ok with me, however, I want you to make choices that really do complete your dreams. Don't let anyone take those dreams away from you or encourage you to go a different direction to what you think you want for yourself. Only you know what is right for you.

Annabella, cherish everyday and live each one to the best of your ability. I'll love you forever no matter what you choose to do or where you choose to go. Where and when you are happy, I will be happy for you.

Hugs and love from
Your Nana

♡ xx oo

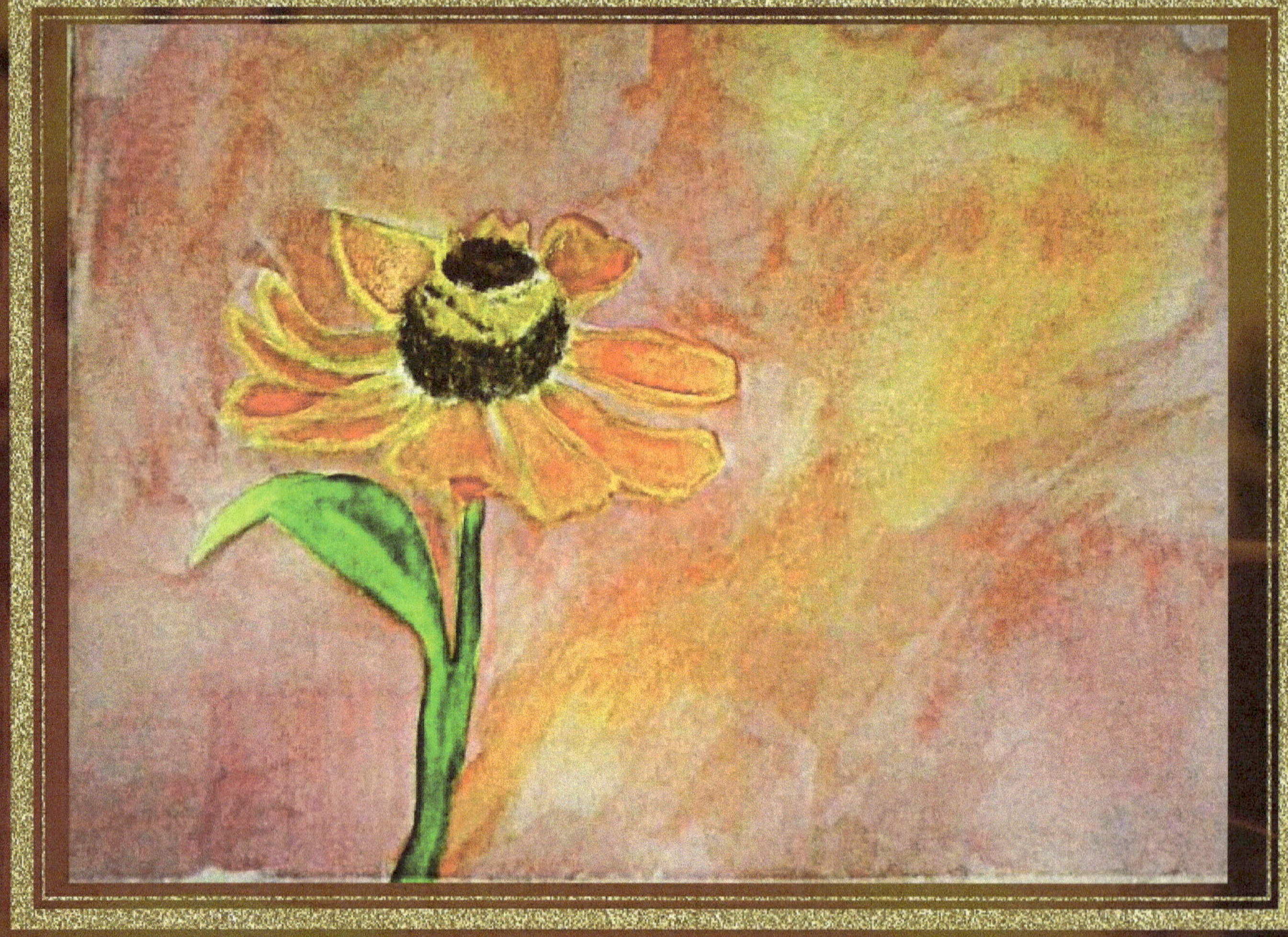

Lisa Tomey-Zonneveld

22

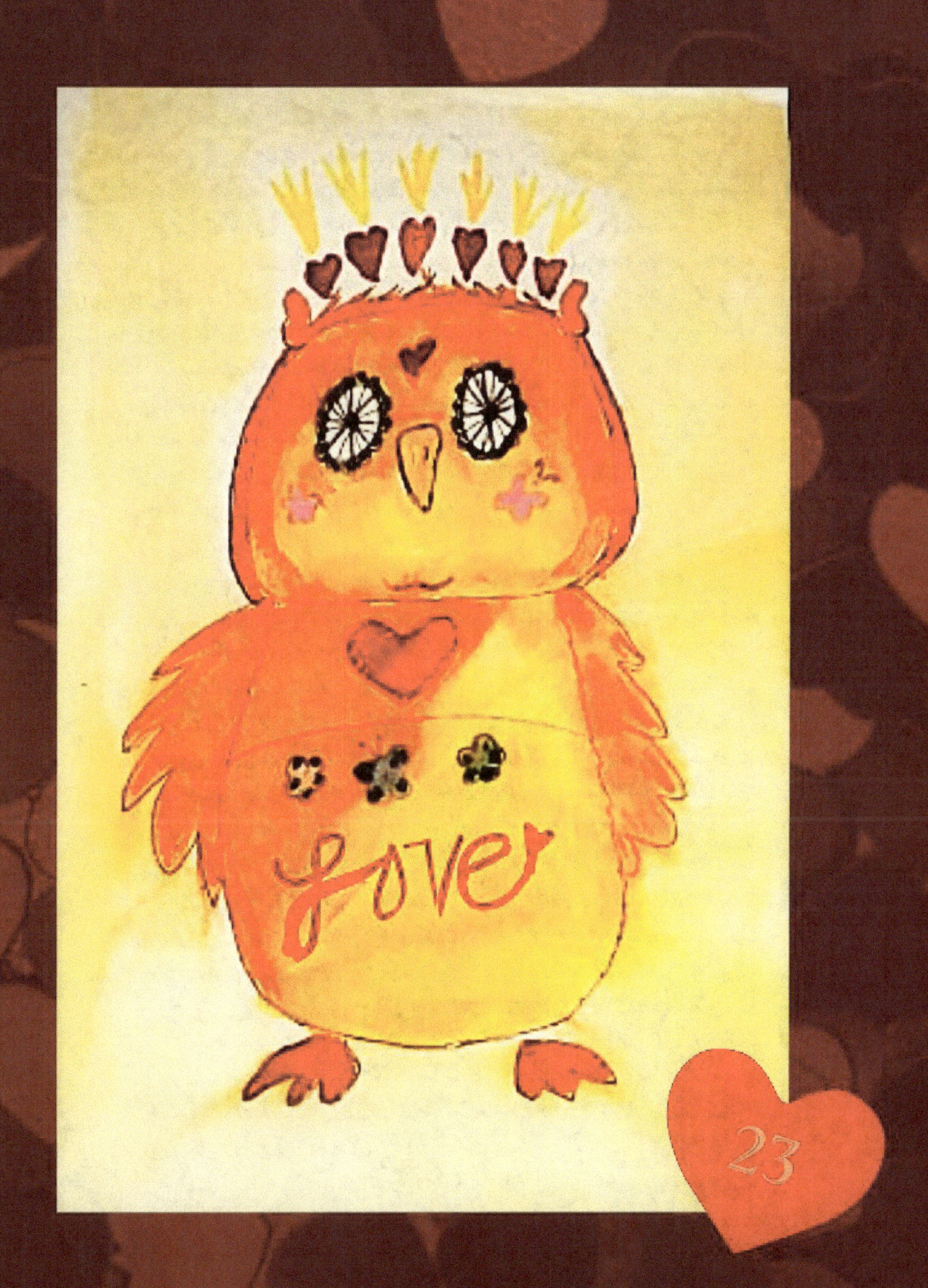
Love

Dear Heart,

I don't need to ask you how you are. I feel you constantly. More important, I see you when you appear to me with your 21 years younger face shines into my days. Your youthful spirit and innocense sparks joy in my life.

My desire is for you to always feel safe. As I live I can keep watch over you, holding vigil with the angels. How to do this when my blood no longer flows? Have I prepared you well enough for this worldly place? I know its a scary place to navigate.

Look at you, though. As you strut your sassy independence you show me your own abilities to ring free. Just be careful about whose hand you hold. I have to trust that lessons have been learned. I also know about vulnerability. Stay in the glow. Charge your spirit. Know your people. Ask yourself if I would trust them with your soul. Hold true to your own stubborn mind. It's the best one I know.

Always know that I am watching you because - NO MATTER WHAT - my spirit will always be alive. With Love -

Nov 14,

PROJECT PLANNING NOTES

Dear Jodi

I Hope that you Like my New Stationary. It's the latest style. Just kidding. I Hear that you are Coming Home For A while. Good. You can Help me Straighten out my Room. It Needs a professional like you are.

I Really Miss you. You've Been my Best Buddy For All your Life. I Think Back at All the Good Times We've Had together in Nauvoo and Here.

I'm slowing up a little bit on my music so that I can get my Eyes and Ears worked on. I Dont Know What's Next.

Hope to See You Soon

Love

Grandpa Max

Max H. Tomey

My Dear Heart,

If I could wave a magic wand and make everything better, I would. I would change the past to make the present and the future what you dream of.

But how, my love, might I make them better? And would it truly be better - or just different? And please let me ask, where else might you want to be now? You've said it yourself many times, 'everything happens for a reason.'

I know you're answers will all include the wish for more - more time, more laughter, more good memories than bad. But again, I cannot change a past that has already been lived.

Nanci Arvizu

You've spent years studying the whats behind the whys and now you know what you know and, you know there is more to learn. This is the journey you are meant to have.

I admire your tenacity. I've seen you throw in the towel a couple of times but only after you have given your all and then some. But I know you love a challenge and the greater the risk, the greater the reward, which sometimes includes the harshest of pain. Having had all those experiences is proof of a well-lived life.

The changes and challenges you are experiencing at this stage of life are not unusual. You are lucky to have the people in your life that you do, especially and specifically right now, to help you over this hump. And really, that is all this moment is; a speed bump on your highway of life. Maybe you should slow down a little so when you hit it, it doesn't send you flying into a ditch. Do that thing you told me to do the year my life was turned upside down — breathe.

I know you have big dreams of how you'd like to live the next twenty or 30 years. It seems like you are attracting opportunities that could make it all happen. I've seen you do it before when you moved your family to another state to live a completely different lifestyle. How happy you were!

If you were to look back at the last 5 years or so, I believe you will find some of those dreams are coming true. The plans you've made are manifesting. I believe this for you!

I carry a rock in my pocket for you. It's small, smooth and shiny, like glass with a golden hue. Every time I touch it I think of you receiving the abundance, success and love you desire.

If I could give one thing to help you through this moment in time - this ending and beginning it would be to just be. Allow things to happen as they should.

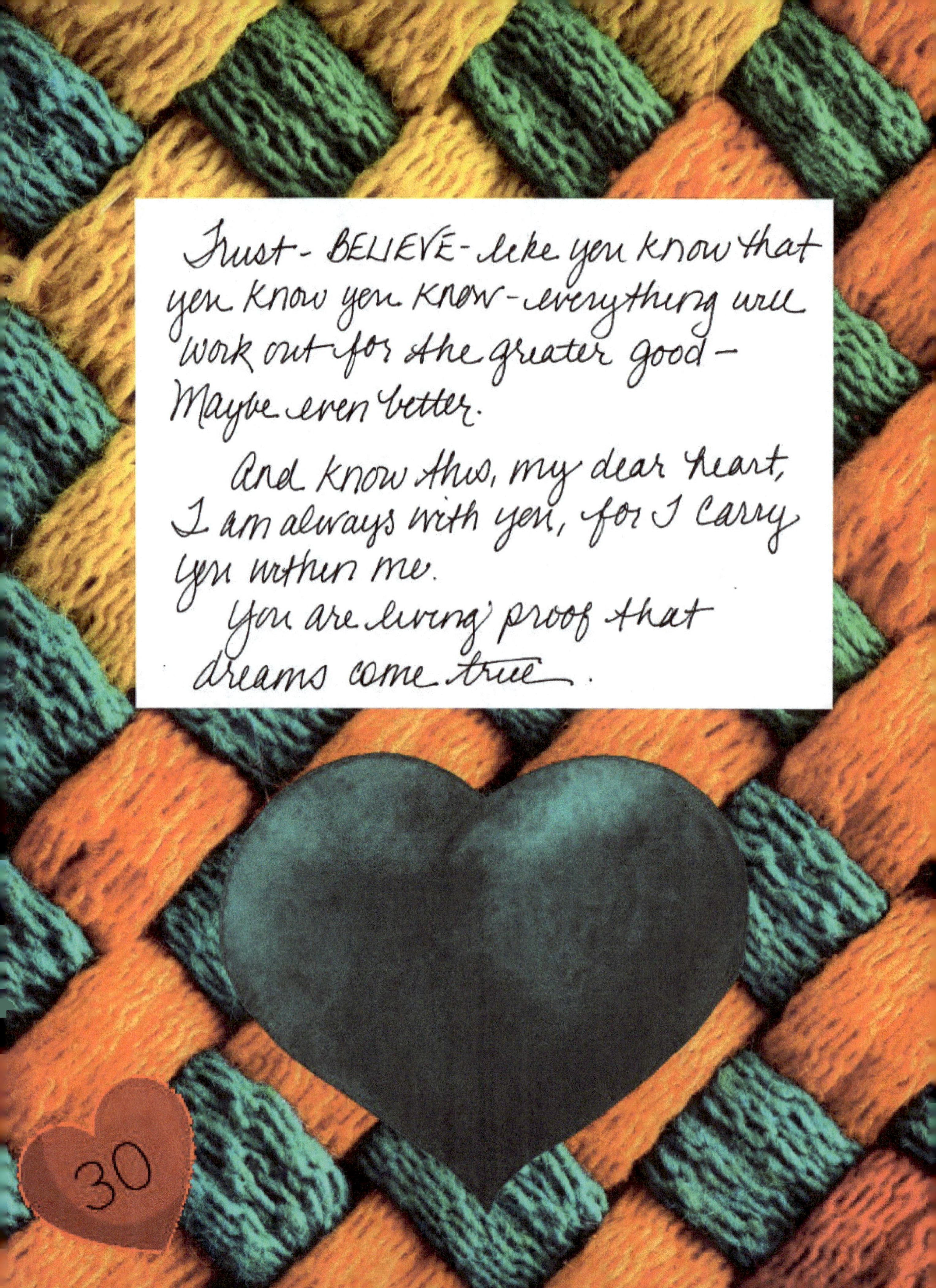
Trust - BELIEVE - like you know that
you know you know - everything will
work out for the greater good -
Maybe even better.
And know this, my dear heart,
I am always with you, for I carry
you within me.
You are living proof that
dreams come true.
30

August 2022

Dear Mum

I wish I could tell you about all the things we have done since you have been gone. Strange, that you were still here this time last year.

I had envisioned us going out on trips and doing activities together - you, me and dad as Eva grew up.

Having time with you so Eva could also share old stories, enjoy activities, visit places, have memories and conversations as she became a woman, like I had the privilege to with my Ma. That is my heart's desire - the three of us, older together and experiencing that bond that I only know too well.

But I am so grateful that you had that chance to meet my little Eva, and although I miss you so much, those photos and videos with you are what I cherish and I will show her as she gets older.

From your loving daughter

Pratibha x

Pratibha Savani

SIDE BY SIDE
Pratibha Savani

side by side
through the years
three generations
stronger together

a warm embrace
a motherly kiss
its the best feeling in the world
we all need times like these

through the years
side by side
a place to come and talk
a place to confide

mum and ma
sharing their wisdom and knowledge
so grateful of having you
both in my life

side · by · side · through · the · years · three · generations · stronger together

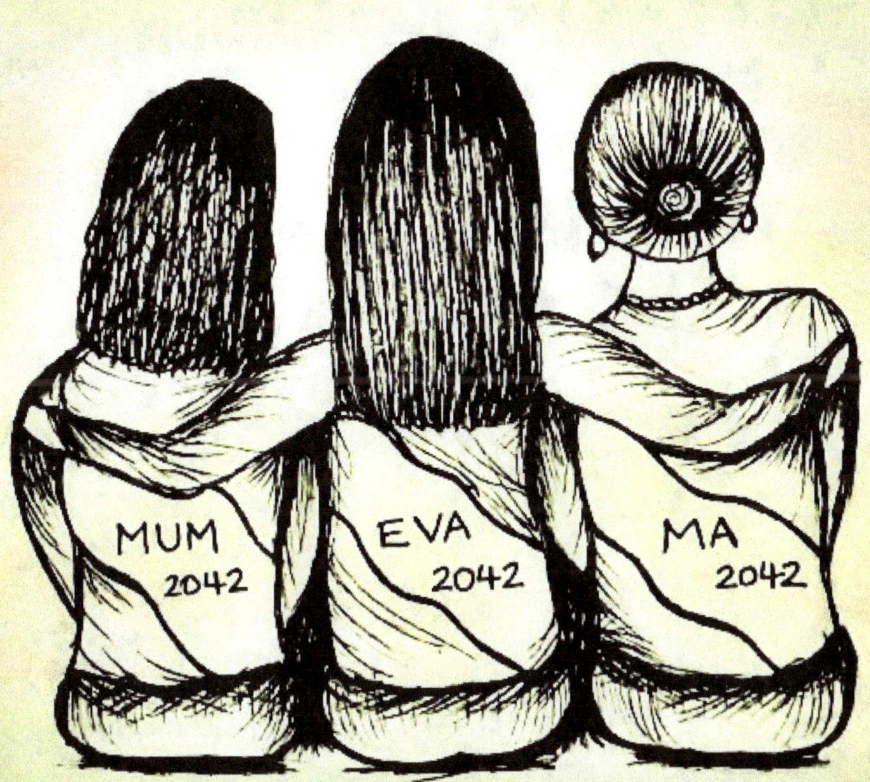

Dear Heart,
what of all this pining
for a child? It's pouring
on another mother's roof.
Another mother's baby rests
in my arm. But I'm growing
strong, strong enough, see?
I am a mother; I am meant
to start my own life. Instead
I am a nanny; I feed
another's infant warm
milk with one hand. In
the other, a plate
& a pen.

Rebecca Herz

Dear Heart,

Were you ever a cold hard lump.
inside my chest, starting out?
Don't deny how you beat with life
spreading red love all over my insides
would you stop and listen now?
Pause in your romance of the unreal?
I just wish to heal
I know you want to go on,
endlessly, to try love and to feel
I do too but sometimes I need
also, a little bit at a time,
to sit with my needles and threads
and mend you, me, all torn parts
soothe and collect your frayed edges
to tuck and sew them into seams of a book
Oh, dear heart! I know the tides
and ebbs of the ocean, you hold inside,
the wrong words that always come out
splintered, broken meanings, dying
with their longing to be 'got'
the ache of knowing, they would not
such hefty pints of sadness to drown
in words again, waiting to be found

Richa Dinesh Sharma

Someone to read and bring to a close
like a chapter, a story, a tale
marks of tears that dried in their trail
for everything to be perfect, not so much
for my smiles to be returned
in the smiling eyes of some,
to be able to say words
that live so blithely inside me
their meanings sleeping safely
in the downy stanzas I write
to feel my echo bouncing off
of other lonely spaces, like me
as my poems are read aloud
from a mouth to an ear
down to the last sob, hiccup
I just mean to be 'got'
for the love shared among many
smiles long sought
all coming down to your beating rhythm
a necessitated need to be prized
to read the letters, the words
and know their meaning deep inside

And, one day, when you are done
buried in sand or burnt to ash

everyone will know that
you and I, we finished better than
when we started out
that' all, dear heart, that really is all
I want us both to ~~be~~ be
well-loved, well-hearted

Sincerely yours
now and forever
You, my dear heart, my balm
and I, your tether.

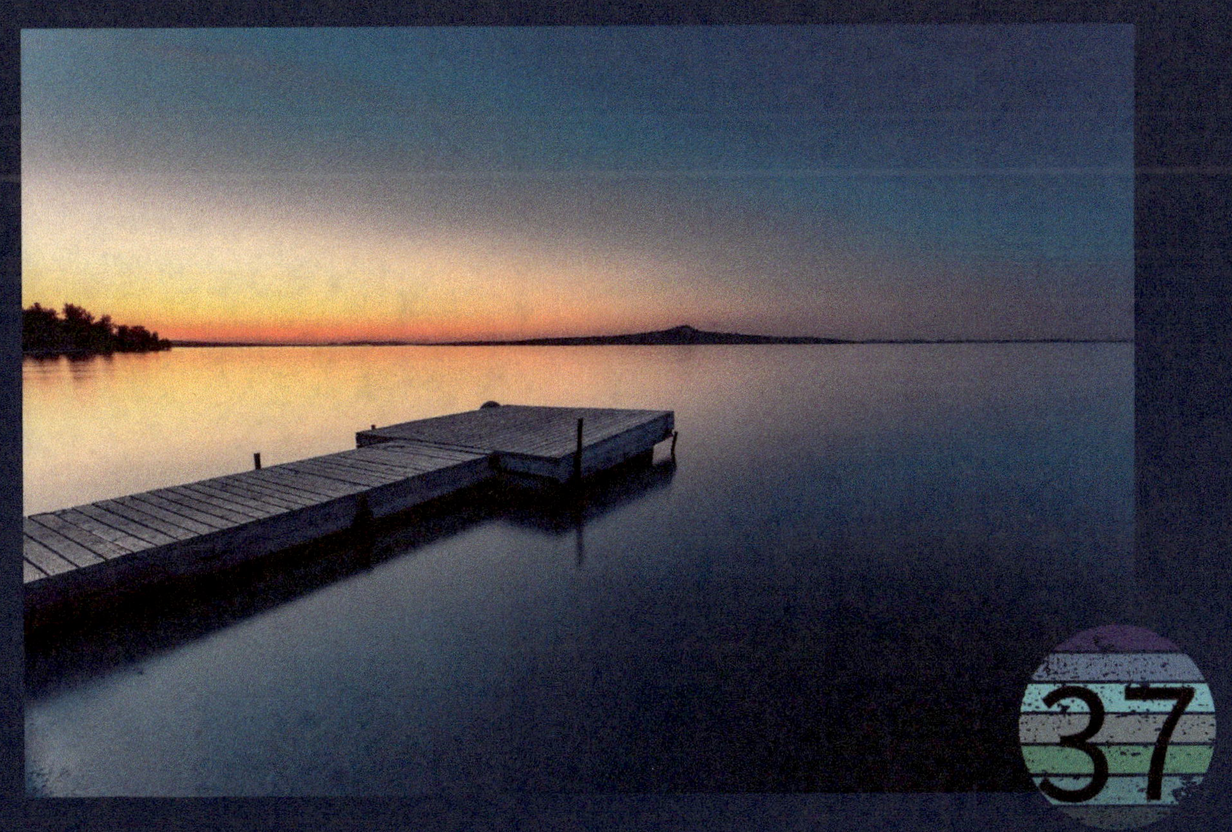

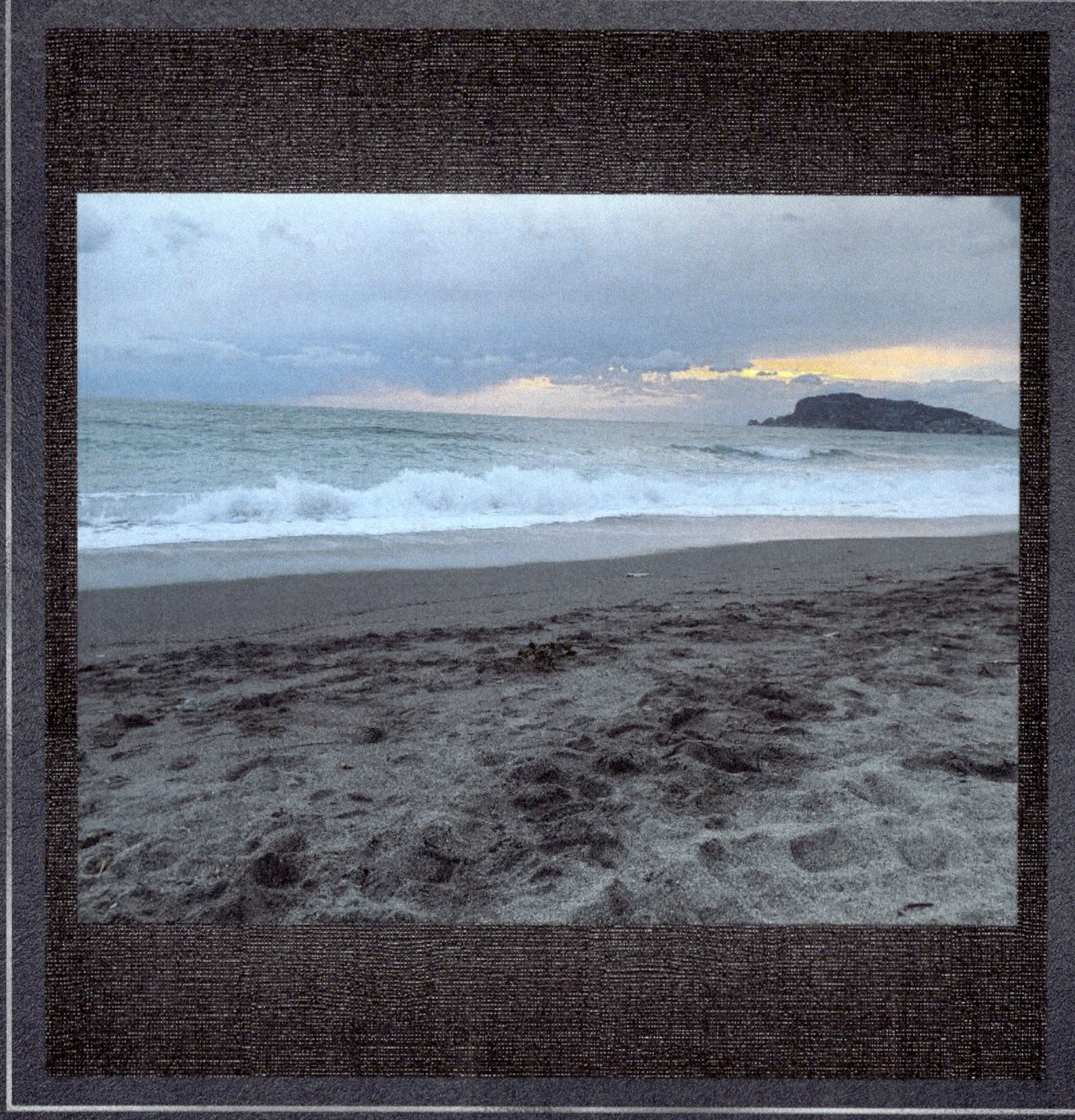

Robin Klammer

38

Turkey - The coast of Alanya

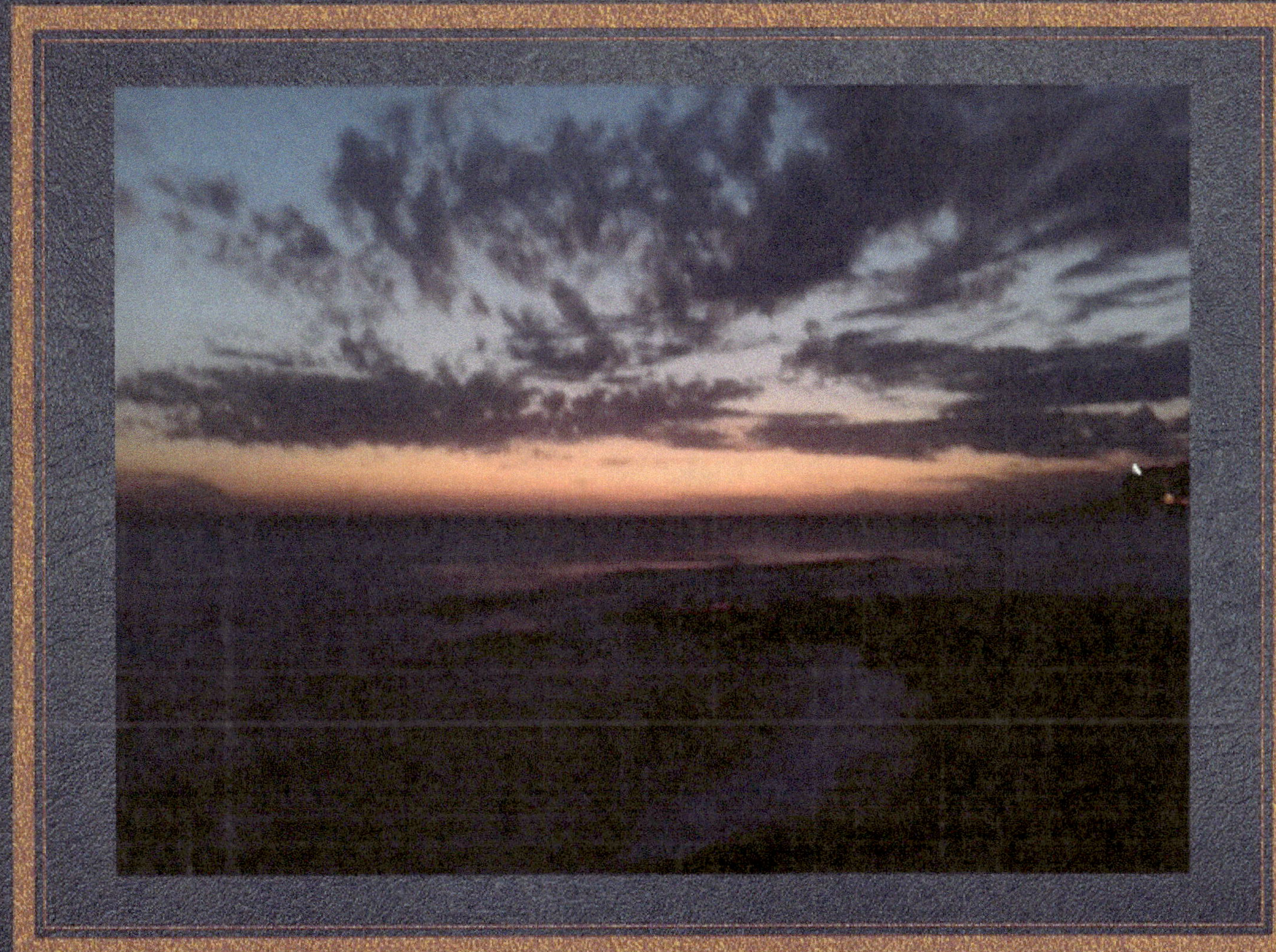

Turkey

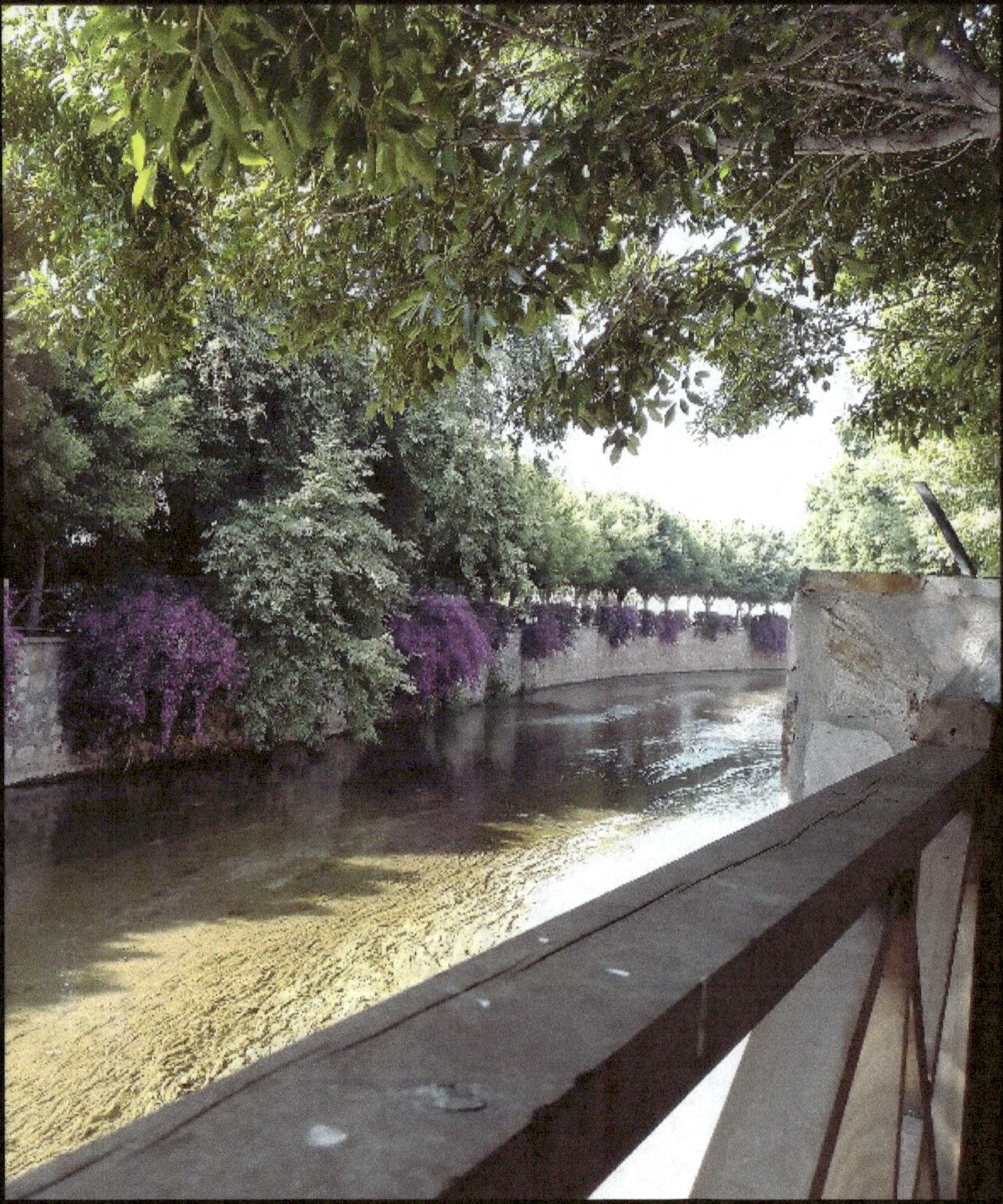

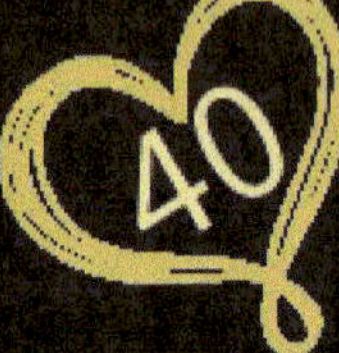

Turkey

Still and Brave

by Sarah Ryan

Dear Heart, where do I start?
Together you and me.
We beat as one again
I missed you for so long.

I knew you were still there
Broken as you were
But I knew you are strong
That you have dreams.

I've followed you for years
Even when your voice is faint.
I listen and wait for my move
Until you tell me to go.

I trust you dearly
You never lead me astray
We are survivors
Your desire has been to save me.

Your desire for me to live my dream
Pushed me forward
Even when I wanted to quit
And the odds were against us.

We are reunited now
You are not only mine anymore
I share you with my sweet son
And my beloved husband.

You keep me praying
Believing and persevering
And now your desire is met
Our dreams together complete.

Thank you, my heart
My still, brave heart that speaks
My guiding light
We made it.

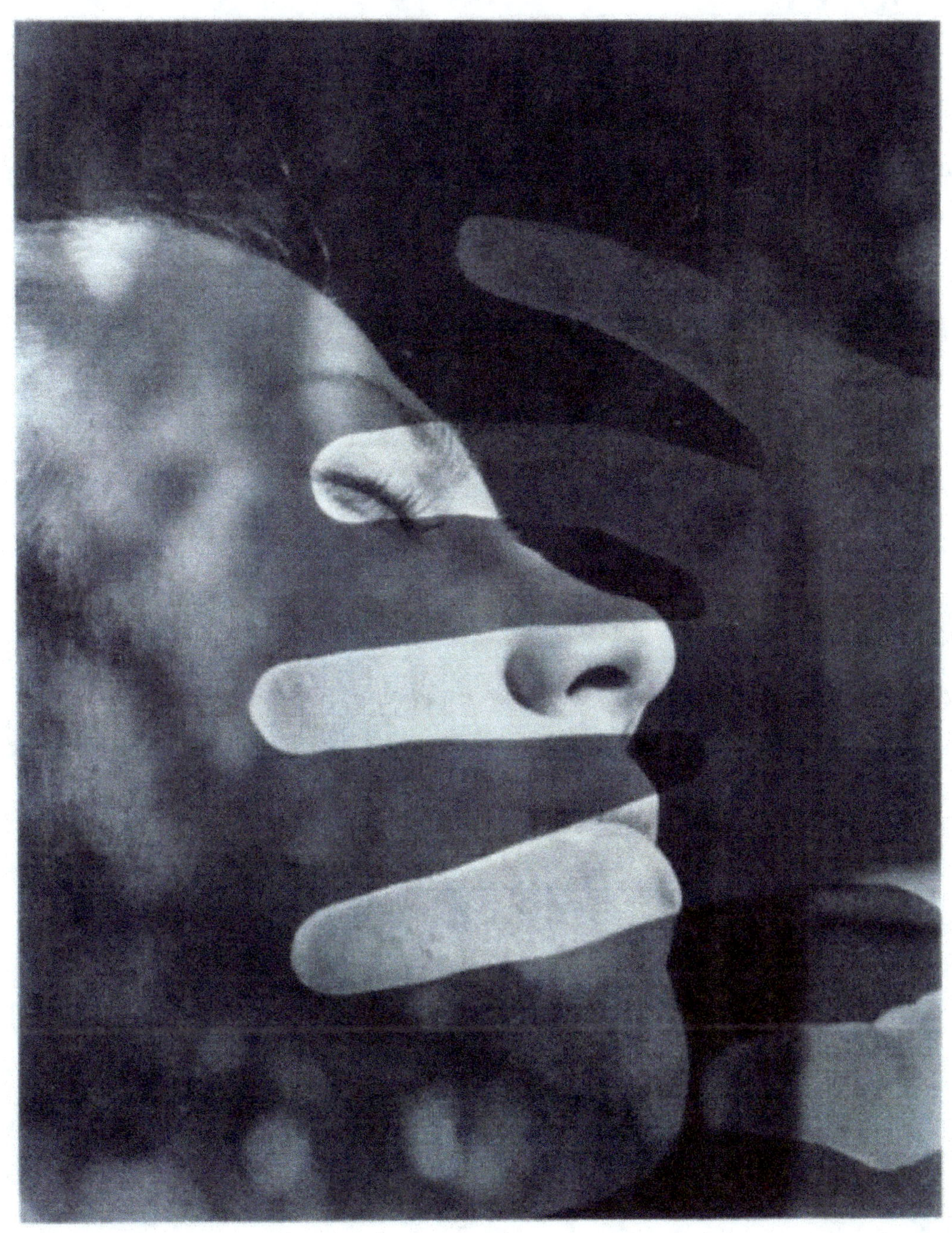

Melancholy

Past lover

My heart yearns for the times,
hand in hand walks aligned,
Trust, honesty, conversational truth,
Bonding together the love of us two,
No other one can embrace my heart,
Balance the beat of its loneliness in part,
Equalize the emotions that completes in rest,
Without having the qualities that our relationship possessed,

How do I
- renouce the thrown of too many broken crowns
- uphold royalty, with the promises profound
- grow apart while keeping lessons taught by you
- Instead of wanting to reverse what split up the love I once knew

Times aging reasons left me contemplating,
Broken hearts severed future congregations,
Holy thou art, to remain with love kept,
Amid the heartbreaking experiences I wish to forget,
Past lover, I invite you to my presence
- so that my future will ever last,

Profound Greetings Broken Heart,

I offer sympathy,
Amid loneliness,
Gestures of Compassion,
Some tear drops missed
Enduring moments of love,
When it feels like pain,
Enlightenment for the darkest exchange,
Of angry conversations when the day has longed,
For embrace, compassions, surronded by nights,
that have wronged,
Engaging moments that love pursued,
After journeyed to another heart to renew
As whole again.

I cry tears of brokeness,
fallen pain exchanged,
Heart felt excruciating hurt in vain,
Loss of integrity, promise admired,
Torn from longevity, heart beats retired,
Its need to hear each other's sound again.

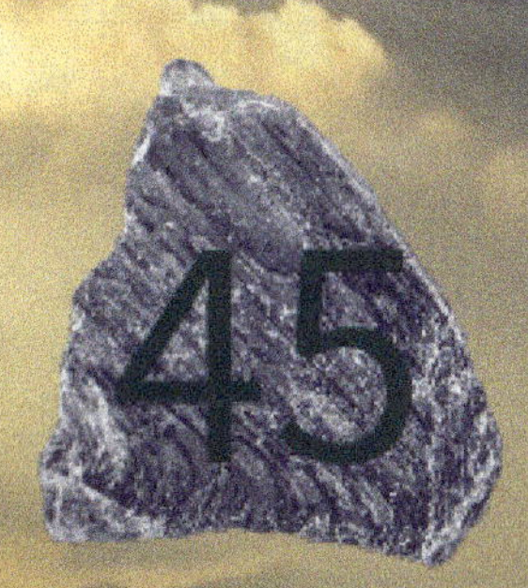

Dearest Heatfelt Emotion,

Numb, I had become without another heartbeat to support the love and emotions that planted themselves inside of me. In a search to find wisdom through the experience's life handed, curiosity left me with a love unknown.

I tried my best to reawaken a heart, that depression left lonely, and pain left without healing any passive time spent building up a strong heart. Researched other's emotions and listened to the sound of their broken reveal. But still felt nothing,

Daily I began to walk down the street, to search for flowers grown from beneath the core of the earth, the dirt, the seeds worth and define a new beginning of my own. I capture the light of sunrises and the meaning of time it set alone.

To many questions in life go unanswered, like what will happen to a coexisting emotion that heatbeats cannot let go of once the relationship has gone its separate ways. With no emotion, I contined my journey while yours ended at the grave.

No longer will I cry tears that loving hands wiped by you, nor listen to your heart that beats loudly while we sleep.

For you and the song you made throughout life must rest in peace.

With no feeling I leave unfamiliar places, that life caused me to drift to. The loss of memory of how I escaped the reminders of what made me blue. Deep down inside, no more cries of loneliness. I vow, to awaken my heart and when I lie dead let it rest without sound.

Forever,

Truest Heart.

DEAR HEART A poem By STEVE ANC

Dear heart,
As I sat within me in search of me...
In search of how to appreciate your patience.
In search of how to encourage you,
I have arrived at the point to say you have tried:

you didn't give up on me.
yes you didn't...
you were there when my feet decided to deny the kne
Even when I matched on the devilish corn,
yet you cool me off.
you have not stared at pain and slide,
Rather you chuck it with ease and bear the hurt.

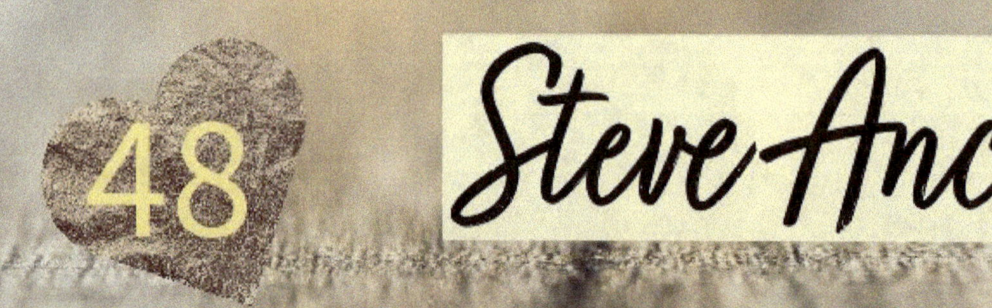

Dear heart,
Thanks for hopping around all day and night---
It is not you desire, but a desire to keep my desires
afloat.

Even as I am awful being.
Sometimes I wished to have hung up hope
Sometimes I wished to have hung up faith
Because hardly a thing could sit in place;
yet you whispered, "Things will sit well!"

Dear heart
life is a leap of faith and sunshine.
Live a life of faith and foresight,
Because your appointed time is near;
Even as the final curtain call to draw
you will draw the best from the well of Life

Dear Friend,

My heart longs to talk with your heart.

My heart recalls the first time our hearts met, cooing back & forth exchanging secrets of the universe.

My heart listened to your heart squeal with delight sharing an umbrella and splashing in puddles.

My heart beams remembering walking through the garden talking about it's okay to be different.

My heart is content after we created friendship bracelets & birdhouses to share with friends.

My heart shines recalling holding

hands on the bus after shopping & giggling at each other's purchases.
My heart rejoiced with the thought of our hearts swaying to the music.
My heart unwinds when our hearts whispers in the quiet, waiting for a fish to bite or watching an eagle soar overhead.
My heart remembers swinging on the front-porch swing, singing songs, & talking about all Mother Nature has to offer.
My heart rests with you around a crackling fire.
My heart yearns to chat with

your heart once again while raking leaves & jumping in them.
My heart smiles with delight remembering chitchatting about future play dates & after dishes were done, finding the North Star.
My heart hums recalling how our hearts felt snuggly warm sharing popcorn while watching a movie.
My heart listened to yours while we sipped tea, waiting for cookies to bake & pinkie-promised our friendship.
My heart chuckles as I think about sharing hot cocoa,

catching snowflakes on our tongues, making snow angels & snowmen for all to see. One day soon, we will swing on the front porch swing while our hearts share all their hopes and dreams. On that day, my heart will leap for joy & all be good with the world again!

Perry Michels

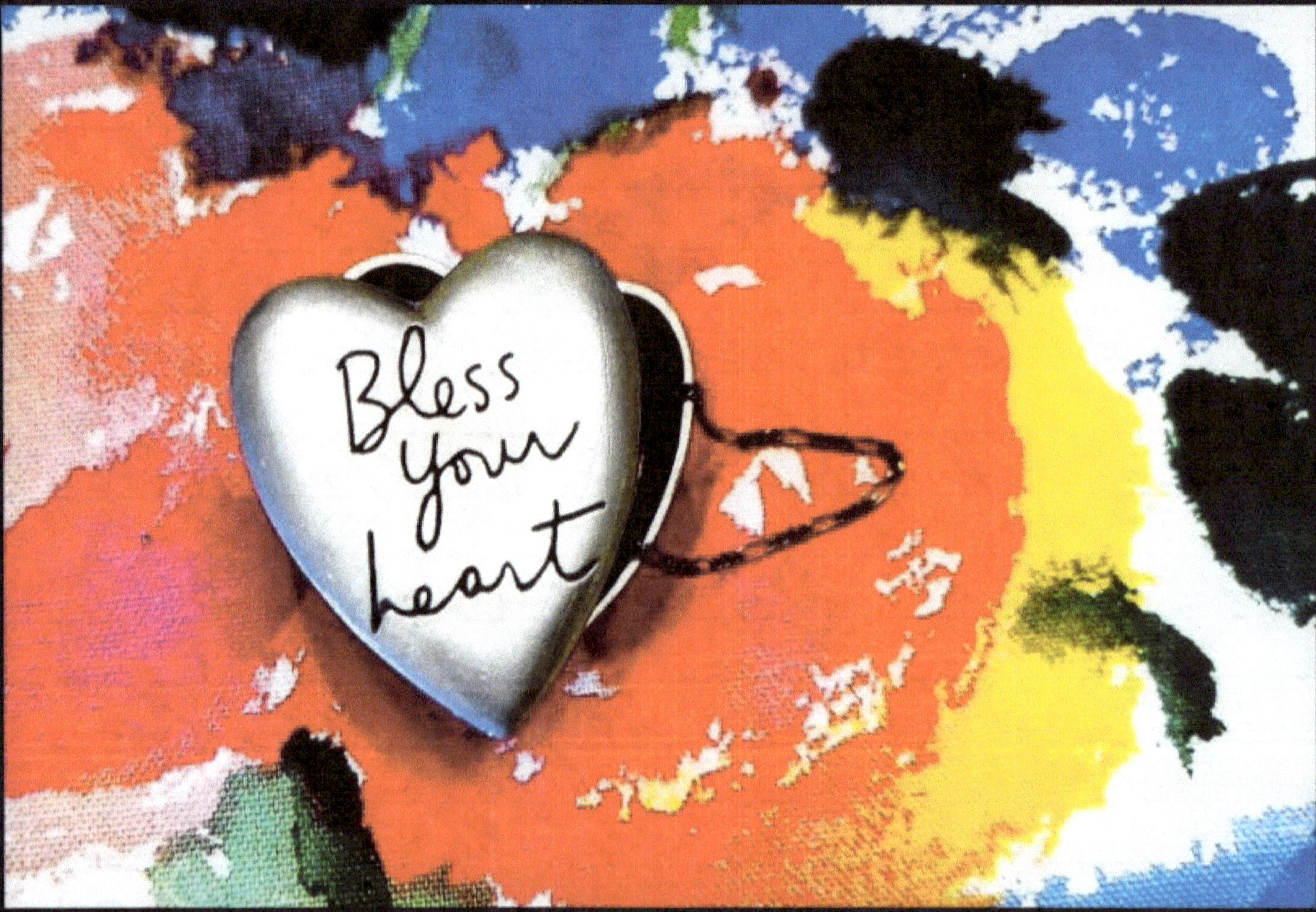

Bless your heart

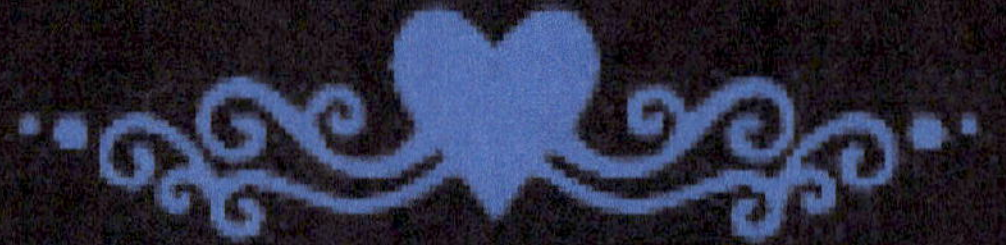

Zan Expressions LLC

ZANETA V. JOHNS

Mother, Tell Me a Story – Yours

If only you could tell me a story
I would pour us a cup of tea
I would settle into a comfy chair
I would give you all of me

I would listen to every single word
Your life story should be heard
Tell me all the juicy good stuff
Tell me about when times were rough

Tell me the wildest of your thrills
What was the worst of your fears
Talk about playing on those red dirt hills
During your Mississippi childhood years

Do share the details of falling in love
Were there combatants you had to shove
Were there suitors you unintentionally hurt
Which songs and scents moved you to flirt

I want your secrets, lessons, and heart's desires
Share any regrets that oft transpired
I know you have a lot to say
Speak slowly, Mother, I have all day

Zaneta Varnado Johns

Dear Universe: August 2022

My heart's desire is to hear my mother's stories. At this stage of my life, I know that her stories would resonate with my own. I want Murr - as we lovingly called her - to tell me what and who made her who she was. How did she become so loving and tolerant despite the challenges she faced? As a young bride and mother, she endured painful losses. I want her sweet voice to tell me how she weathered those storms. What made her tick, beside her infinite love for us? How was she able to make each of us feel like the most loved, most special, most unique? Did God create her this way? If only she were here to answer these questions - to tell me a story - if only!

Together we would travel to her childhood days in Mississippi. Deep-rooted in red dirt, her grit would be revealed in stories of wonder. Her 20th century journey would include her arrival at Hammond Colored High School in Louisiana. It was there that she excelled as an honor student and fell in love with my tall, dark and handsome daddy. I would ask her about the note she wrote in his senior memory book that read, "... follow your heart ..." My imagination wants to fill in the blanks. I get goosebumps thinking about my young mother writing that note to my will-be father. The fact that he listened warms my heart even more!

If you're open to my request, please know that I would listen attentively to my mother's stories. My heart would rejoice with my dream-come-true. I would speak only when necessary. I would not judge. I would ask about her creative muse and unspoken interests. I would carefully note any secrets or lessons or wisdom—subtle or direct. I would ask follow-up questions to pursue details. I know that Mom would be content, simply to be heard. Her voice mattered. Her joys, pains and lessons mattered! Moreover, my mother's heart's desire—to share her stories—mattered!

Murr passed away unexpectedly in 2000, one day after her Birthday. I carry her safely in my heart, but too many of her life's stories I missed. I also missed the opportunity to share my own grown-up stories with her. A couple weeks before she passed, my mother wanted to teach me how to cook her delicious chicken-and-dumplings. I took a raincheck, to my regret! My ultimate heart's desire is to sit and listen to my mother's stories, hopefully while eating a plate of chicken-and-dumplings — lovingly and joyfully prepared by just us two!!! ♡♡

With love and hope,

Zan

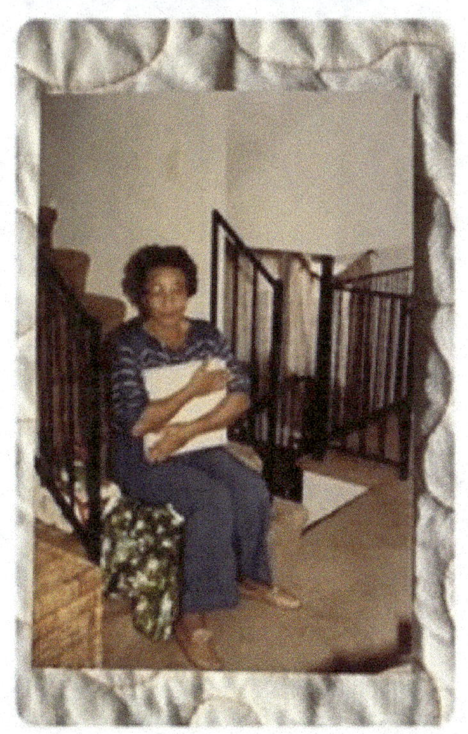

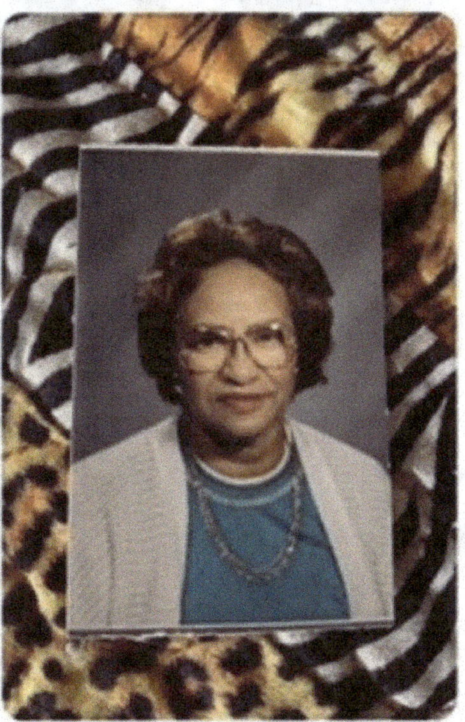

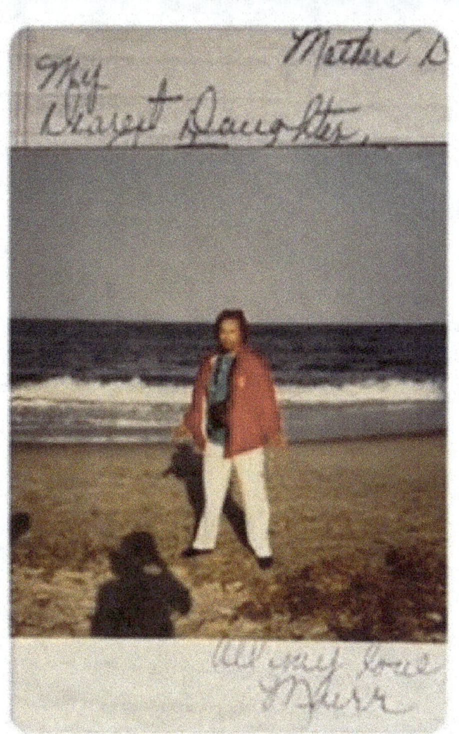

A U T O B I O G R A P H Y

My name is Benice Lea Bonds Varnado. I was born in Liberty, Mississippi on August 14, 1931 to Bennie and Marie Bonds. I spent my early childhood with my aunt and uncle, Mr. and Mrs. Tomey Brumfield, Sr. in Osyka, Mississippi. There I attended school from first to eighth grade. My high school years were spent in Hammond, Louisiana where I lived with my mother and stepfather so that I could attend high school. I graduated from Hammond Colored High School in 1948 with honors.

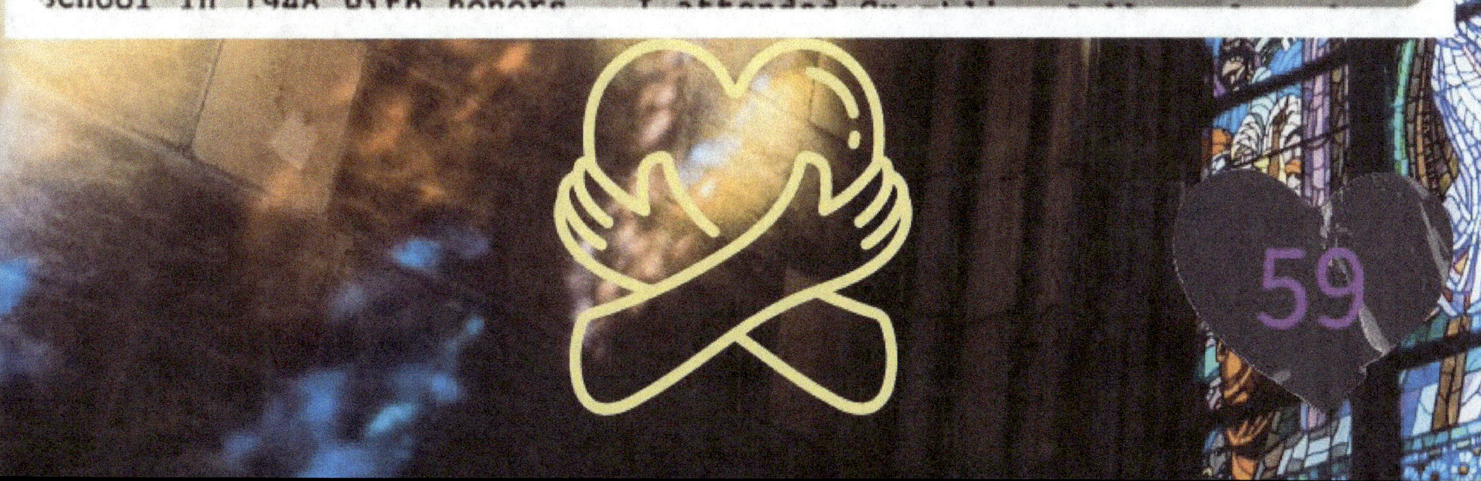

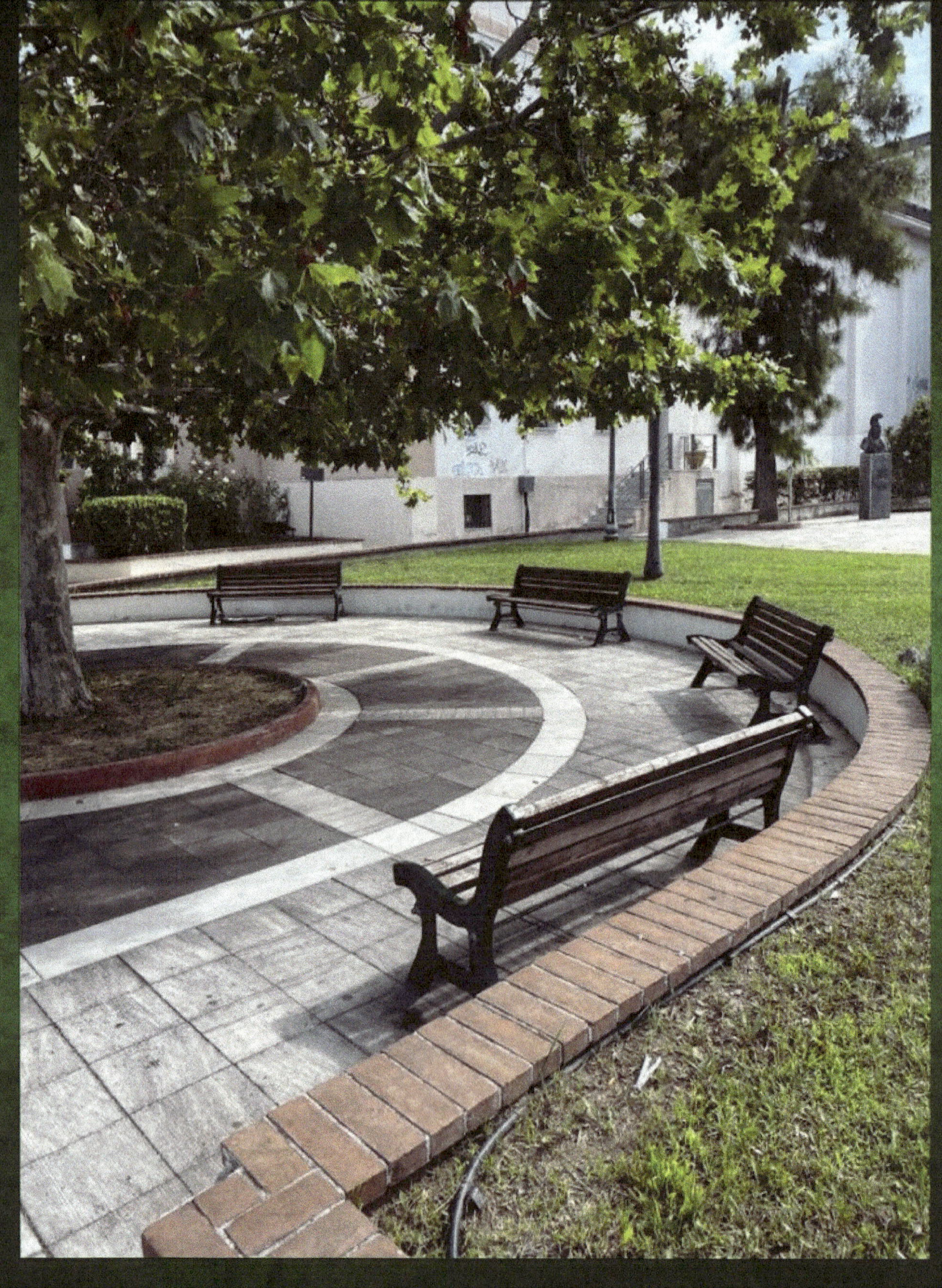

benches from Greece trip 2023

Gratitude for all the helpers who made this dream book happen:

Zaneta Varnado Johns for her excellent line editing skills, with the strongest "Eagle Eyes" I have ever known.

Jodi Lynn Nehring, my dear daughter and partner in crime, helped me with all the scans and added her own special touches.

Kay Doiron, my dear great niece whom I always rely upon for her magical cover art. She "gets" me every time.

And to all the wonderful contributors to *Dear Heart*:

Steve Anc is a Nigerian poet, searching knowledge and deep meditation on universal themes. Anc's works have been published by Prolific Pulse Press LLC, *OpenDoor Magazine, Poetrysoup, Goodlitcompany, Voice from The Void, Our Poetry Archive, I Become the Beast, Fire Magazine, South Broadway Press,* and *Phoenix Z Publishing.*

Nanci Arvizu is an author, speaker, podcaster, and tech lover with nomadic dreams. Her poetry and essays are published in *A Safe and Brave Space* (2021 & 2022), *Fine Lines Journal* (2021), *Social Justice Inks* (2022), and *Speak Magazine* (2022). Arvizu's fiction and non-fiction e-books are available on Amazon.

Kay Doiron, Dear Heart cover artist, resides in Alabama with a paintbrush in one hand and toys in the other. Her heart beats for her three beautiful children.

Rebecca Herz is the author of *Homecoming*. Her individual poems can be found in *Sinister Wisdom Journal, The Last Leaves, The Madrigal, Fine Lines,* and on *Medium.* Rebecca is a graduate student of social work at Rutgers University and lives in New Jersey with her wife and cats. You can follow Rebecca on Medium (@homecoming poet).

Chyrel J. Jackson grew up in a Southern Suburb of Chicago, IL. She was influenced by amazing Black writers like James Baldwin, Toni Morrison, Langston Hughes, and Sonia Sanchez. Jackson and her sister, Lyris D. Wallace, published *Mirrored Images* and *Different Sides of the Same Coin*, modern collections of poetry. Website: SistersRocnRhyme.com

Zaneta Varnado Johns is a Pushcart Prize nominee and bestselling author of *Poetic Forecast* and *After the Rainbow: Golden Poems*. She is a co-author in *Voices of the 21st Century (2021, 2022, & 2023)*, co-editor of *Social Justice Inks* anthology and will release the *What Matters Journal* in Summer 2023. An editor of the *Fine Lines Journal*, Johns contributes to numerous international anthologies and poetry publications. Website: zanexpressions.com

Jill Sharon Kimmelman has been nominated twice for the Pushcart Prize. Recent publications include *Vita Brevis Press, Spillwords Press, Fine Lines, Love of Food*, and multiple anthologies. She published *You Are the Poem*, a three-themed debut collection of poetry, art, and photography in 2021. Passions: Reading aloud, cooking, photography, and theatre. Kimmelman lives in Delaware USA with her husband Tim and is the proud mother of her son Jordan.

Robin Klammer is a Canadian writer. Just give her a stack of books, good coffee and sustenance, and she's good to go! Klammer is an avid bookworm for life! She is a writer on *Medium* and contributor to several publications including poetry anthologies. Dark humor is her go-to in life.

Danielle Martin is a Trinidadian poet/writer whose work can be found in various online and book publications. She is the author of *Sweet Talk: Caribbean Culture* and *Kissing Shadows: Caribbean Love Poems*, both of which are available on Amazon for your reading pleasure.

Terri DeGezelle Michels is an author and photographer who has published more than 60 children's non-fiction titles. Her latest fiction title, *Simon of Cyrene, the Legend of the Easter Egg*. Terri shares her writing experiences during school visits where she encourages students to follow their dreams. Terri's passions include traveling, reading, and writing.
Website: TerriMichels.com

Karen E. Monteith lives, writes, reads, does needlework, and enjoys her family in Barrie, ON, Canada. Karen is writing two books, a cookbook requested by family and a book on the healing benefit of the needle-arts. You can find her writing on Medium.com @Karenemonteith or on her blog Karenmonteith.com

Jodi Lynn Nehring is from Raleigh, North Carolina. She loves to create greeting cards, work on puzzles, sew, listen to music, talk to friends, travel, attend church, and watch "Supernatural" and TV police shows.

Sarah Ryan is a North Carolina native who has had a lifelong passion for creative writing through poetry, creative nonfiction, and memoir. Her poetry has been published through Whispering Angels Books and PurpleStone Press. She finds her creative spark through nature, faith, and reflection.

Pratibha Savani is a UK Poet, Artist, and author of *Tangles + Knots*. Published in *OpenDoor Magazine* and in several anthologies, she is a creative soul, inspired by the cosmos, nature, and spirituality. Pratibha likes to defy the rules with her inventive expressions on Instagram and Facebook: Pratibha Poetry Art.

Shiela Denise Scott, nominated award winning poet published in multiple languages, anthologies, and magazines, delves into the art of writing. Scott, with an earned B.A.A. in Creative Writing, looks to entertain the art connoisseurs. Follow her on social media: Facebook, Shiela Denise Scott and Twitter, Shiela Denise.

Richa Dinesh Sharma lives in Singapore with her husband, two human children, and one furchild. Her poems are featured in journals *Fine Lines*, *OpenDoor Poetry* magazine, *Our Poetry Archives,* and some anthologies. She also published an essay in *The Talk.* Occasionally, as inspiration strikes, she writes in Hindi, "Hindi fostered my love of reading and writing while English indulged me like an aunt."- She dabbles in Art when not writing or daydreaming. At present, she is working remotely as an editor of the reputed quarterly *Fine Lines Journal.* On Instagram: @dryink_brush

Alice Taylor writes memoir based on childhood trauma, grief, and life experiences, sprinkled with writing perspectives. She is passionate about mastering the craft of writing. As a certified life coach, her mission is to touch hearts, inspire writers, and encourage dreams by helping aspiring writers write their memoir.

Max H. Tomey, U.S.A.F Retired, resting at his Heavenly home. Known as "Daddy" to publisher Lisa Tomey-Zonneveld, this remarkable man wrote the published letter to his granddaughter Jodi. She chose to share his expression of love which speaks well to their close grand relationship.

Jia-Li Yang (Cassa Bassa) resides in Sydney, Australia. She blogs at FlickerofThoughts.com Her work has been published in the *Australian Poetry Journal; The Poets Symphony, Creation and the Cosmos* published by Raw Earth Ink; *Heart Beats, Social Justice Inks* published by Prolific Pulse Press LLC; Wounds I Healed published by EIF.

Lisa Tomey-Zonneveld is the founder and manager of Prolific Pulse Press LLC and a widely published poet and writer. Her most recent publication is *Caring for Souls*. She is the editor of numerous anthologies and serves as an editor of the *Fine Lines Journal*. Tomey- Zonneveld served as the Poet Laureate of the Garden of Neuro Institute. She resides in Raleigh, North Carolina.

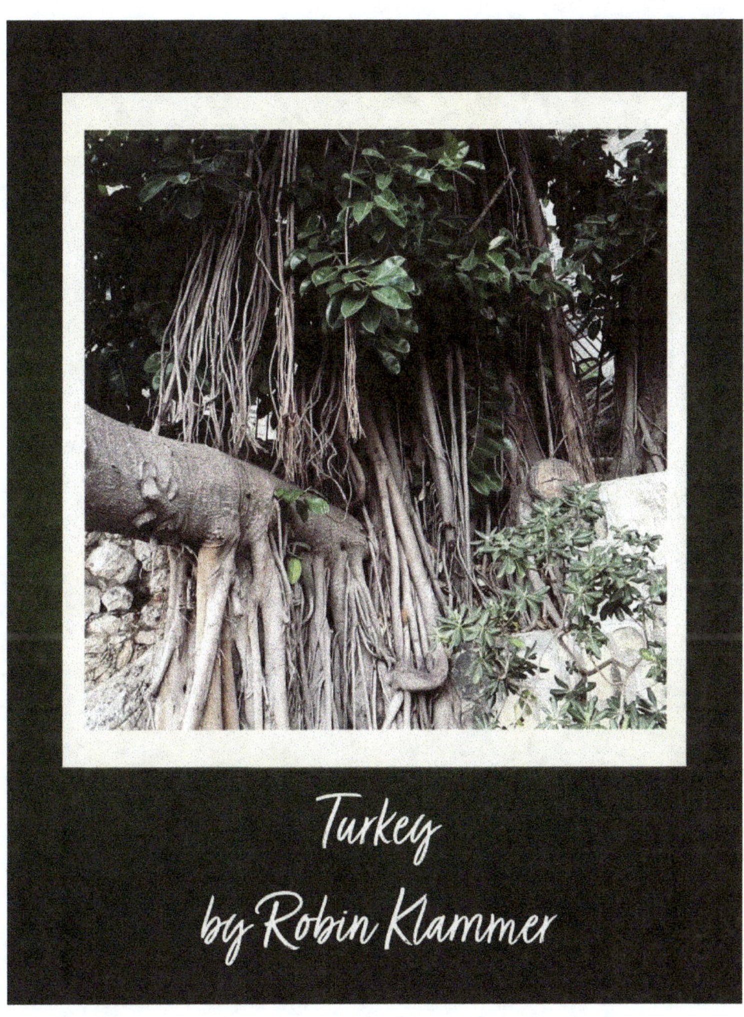

Now, it's your turn to write a letter, poem, dedication, essay, draw a picture, paste a photograph, all to express the desires of your heart.

Next are some journal or letter writing pages and there a couple of blank pages at the end of the book for doodling or adding art and/or photos.

If you choose to participate in this activity we would love to see what you have created.

Feel free to send your finished work to prolificpulse@gmail.com with "Heart's Desire" on the Subject line.

Be sure and check out the latest from Zaneta Varnado Johns.

There's more to come from this prolific poet!

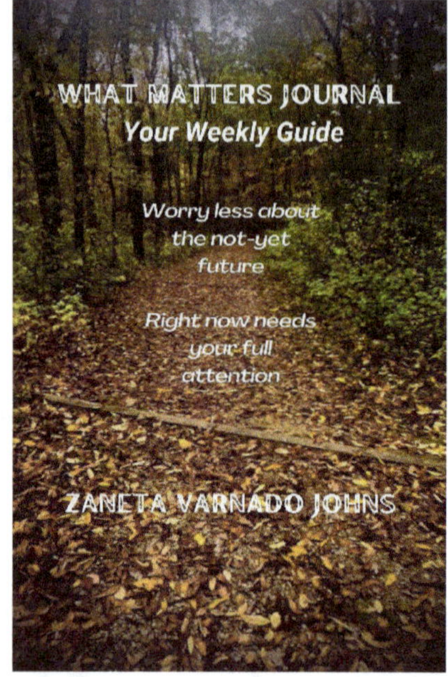

ZanExpressions.com

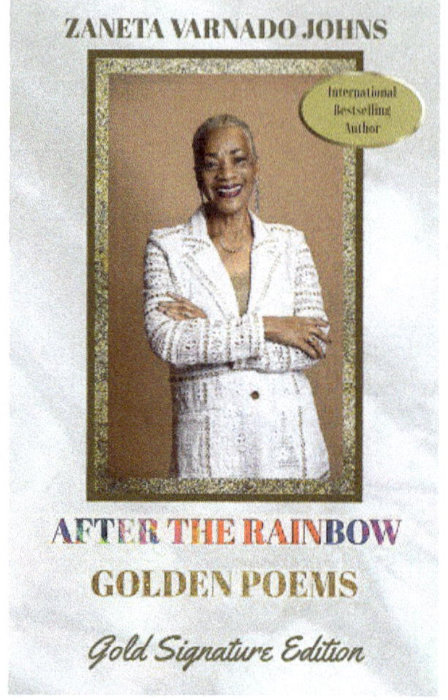

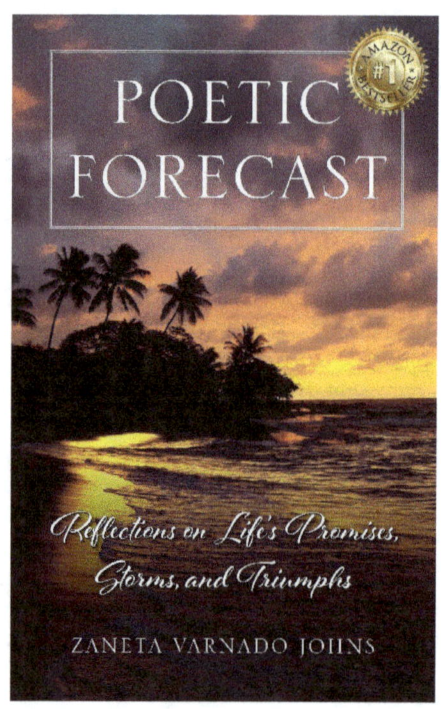

Are you interested in learning about future anthologies?

Be sure to check out our website for updates.

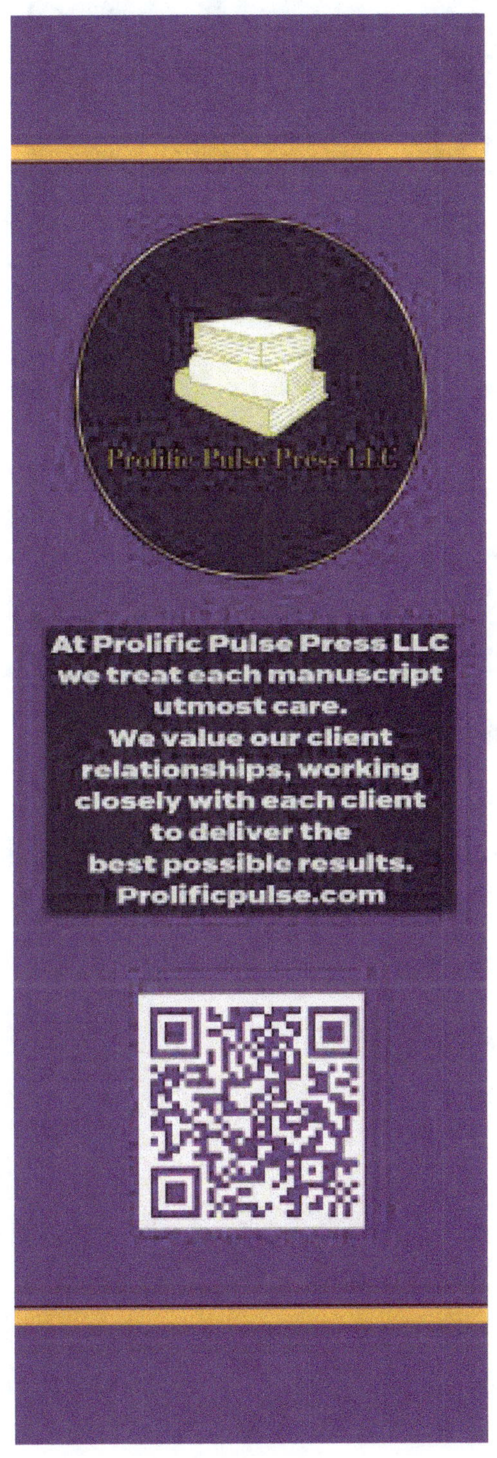

Other Anthologies by Prolific Pulse LLC

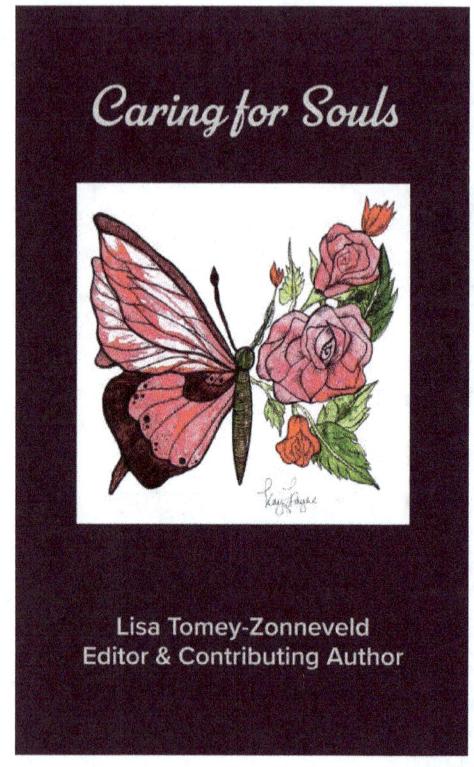

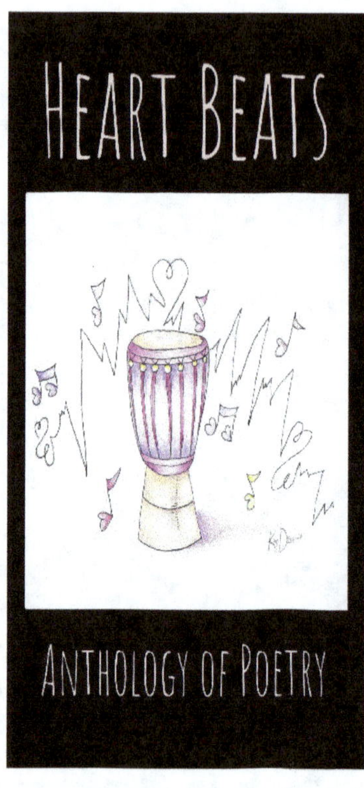

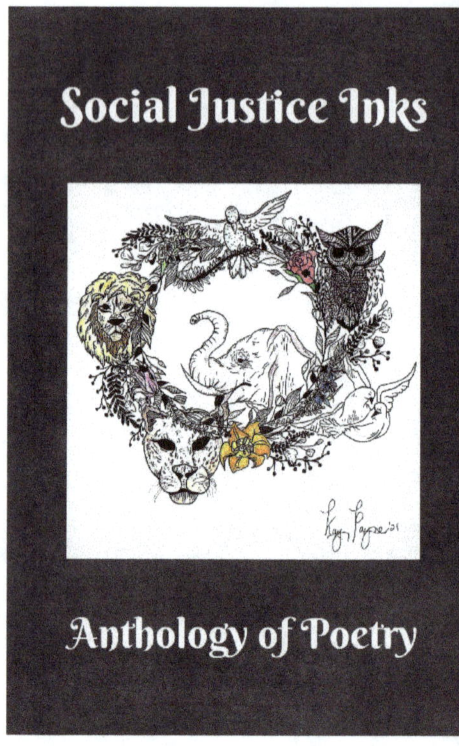

Announcements for the 2024 Anthology will be Released by December 2023

www.ingramcontent.com/pod-product-compliance
Lightning Source LLC
LaVergne TN
LVHW081634120826
845149LV00025B/1909
* 9 7 8 1 9 6 2 3 7 4 0 2 6 *